Halt Sucker!

A TPD Corporal's Official Memoirs
Corp Joseph A. Severino

PRESENTED TO

J. A. Severino

FOR OUTSTANDING
AND DEDICATED SERVICE
3-23-65 TO 1-10-78

F.O.P.A. LODGE NO. 39
DEAN CARY,
PRESIDENT

Halt Sucker!

A TPD Corporal's
Official Memoirs
Corp. Joseph A. Severino

Printed December 2021

Published by
PGP Publishing

Formatting & Illustration by
John S. Nagy

Editing by
John S. Nagy &
Kenneth B Gibson

ISBN 13: 979-8-7845686-1-8

Dedication

Although this collection of stories seems to belong to me personally, be assured that I did not collect them by myself. For each story or described incident I had at least one or more accomplices. Some of my co- conspirators are named. Some will not be mentioned.

When you see a reflection of yourself in these many stories, I hope each may bring back memories that make you smile and maybe reminisce about the good times we all enjoyed traveling the law enforcement highway together.

These writings are dedicated to the men and women who made it happen, both sworn and civilian.

Thank you all for sharing your lives with me and making me richer for what you brought to mine.

Corporal Joseph A. Severino
22 March 1965 – 01 January 1978

Preface

This is a rendition of a humble but very exciting book containing episodes which occurred during my career as a Tampa Police Department employee. It may seem as if it were a made up fantasy but it has been said and attested to by brothers and sisters who actually lived the story: "Man, you can't make this crap up!"

During most of our careers even the common cold couldn't keep us from reporting for work. This job brought so much sense of doing good and of being there in the thick of what might happen on our next shift.

My spouse said to me several times, "Honey, stay home. You are not feeling well."

My answer always was, "I gotta go to work. Last night the elephants showed up. Hell, the clowns may show up tonight."

This collection of my memories is in every way a collection of events and happenings that bonded our department and, more especially, our squads. We were a tight-knit group of men and women that formed friendships that have lasted beyond mere days, weeks, months, or years – *some that have lasted decades.*

Please read this with the understanding that it has been written to reflect my thanks to all who helped me mentally, physically, emotionally, and spiritually during my travels in the Law Enforcement environment.

I

And So It Begins

What occurs when a twenty-three year old young man and a friend decide to leave the college life and join the Tampa Police Department in March 1965?

This chapter shares stories as close as possible about my journeys from March 1965 through to January 1978.

Here it goes!

Passing the Test

A recently discharged US Marine named Michael and I decided to join the Tampa Police Department. Back then the process was not complicated. One merely applied at the Department, they sent you to an interview, then a physical – which consisted of a visit to a doctor who was contracted to perform the screening which wasn't very extensive. It consisted of a mere physical examination, blood work, and a urine test for drugs. When this exam was completed, they either accepted you or rejected you.

Well during this process, several police candidates and fire department applicants were to meet the doctor's office for said test. On that bright morning the applicants were rounded up in group fashion and provided a glass vial in which to deposit our urine samples. I guess in an attempt to hurry the process along we all went into the men's room to give the sample.

One of the fire department candidates decided to act silly. The young man washed his beaker with soap and water. He then filled the beaker with tap water. When the elderly nurse came in to obtain the samples, this clown announced that he thought his sample appeared weak. To the elderly nurse's dismay, he held the beaker up, proclaimed that he thought he would recycle the sample, and proceeded to drink from the beaker.

That prank almost ended the beginning of our careers.

Thank God the Doctor had a sense of humor.

On Patrol

So, this began our careers in both departments.

After a short stint in a Police Academy at 1710 Tampa Street, we were released upon the citizens of Tampa Florida. We were assigned to either a traffic or patrol squad and it was a crapshoot as to which one you landed in.

I was fortunate to be assigned to a patrol squad.

After being introduced to a senior patrolman who was going to show us how to be a police officer, I was told that my job was to ride and observe, to forget anything I was taught in the "Academy", and that he would teach me everything I needed to know to succeed.

I was to be seen and not heard, learn to take notes, write reports and to speak only when spoken to. Trying to keep my job, I really tried to follow directions as best I could. I was raised in Tampa Florida and I thought I knew a lot for my young age.

I remember one call to the Ponce DeLeon Public housing project about one am on a Saturday night. We were met at the first floor front door by a black lady in a highly excited state who urged us to come upstairs with her. On the way up the stairs, I could smell the odor of what I thought could have been gun powder. Upon closer examination I saw two scrape marks on the wall which were later identified as gun shots.

The lady was complaining that her teenage son had physically hit her and that she had fired two shots at him as he ran down the staircase. The son was still present and his mother exclaimed that if we didn't take this N___er with us right then, she would call Ray Williams next time.

Being a good rookie, I stayed true to my instruction and kept quiet, listening and taking mental notes in case I had to write something down.

After returning to our police cruiser empty handed I broke my silence and asked, "Okay, who the hell is Ray Williams?"

I was taken by surprise to learn that Ray Williams was a popular and well known black undertaker in Tampa.

We likely saved this young man's life.

My Initiation

After making it through a learning process and passing the muster as to whether or not I could handle the job, I was placed in a patrol car with two older career police officers who really didn't meet up to the standards of what I thought model policemen should be. Both were way over weight, smoked cigars, and were acting as if they didn't give a damn about anything.

Unknown to me, I was going to be tested as to whether I would fight or run. I weighed about one hundred and forty pounds soaking wet and was skinny as a rail.

When driving down Franklin Street south from the Police Station about three pm we entered Skid Row. It was a very undesirable part of downtown where pawn shops, bars and tattoo parlors were located. The police car abruptly stopped and the officers pointed to a large man standing on the sidewalk not bothering anyone.

They directed me to arrest said man for being drunk as he was always drunk, they even knew his given name, *Carsile Wilkins*. He was a painter by trade. Desiring to get these officers to return a good report on me I attempted to do their bidding. I walked up to Carl and told him he was under arrest for being drunk and to place his hand on the wall.

The officers failed to tell me a very important fact about this massively large man. They didn't tell me that *he was cooperative as long as you didn't try to man-handle him or put your hands on him in any way.*

As soon as I touched him he went berserk. He was so strong that he had me flying off my feet like a flag in the wind. Eventually the two overweight Cops came to my aid and the Giant was subdued.

Guess I passed the fight or flight test.

During my career I knew several officers that were hired that never passed that exam.

Beat Characters

Walking the beat became a part of my career which I really enjoyed. As a beat officer you got to meet and interact with the different characters who made up the populace of skid row: the owners of the businesses, the drunks, whores, pick pockets, and derelicts.

One of the colorful people there was *Stoney*, the owner of the bar "Big Mary". He was an older man who operated a tattoo parlor. Stoney was from Tennessee and suffered from dwarfism. He was a hell of an artist and a Carney-type of person.

There was also Robert Chester, known as *Scooter*. He was the inventor of the first skateboard. Scooter was missing both of his legs. He had roller skate wheels attached to a board and he used a piece of four by four with a rubber surface to propel his skate board forward. Robert many times would get sloppy drunk and fall off his ride. If anyone, including, a Cop, tried to help him, he would attempt to hit them with his four by four.

Call Boxes

The skid row beats were manned twenty-four hours a day, in three shifts a day, 7 am to 3 pm, 3 pm to 11 pm, and 11 pm to 7 am. The only mode of communicating on these beats was by the use of a cast iron box referred to as a call box.

It was necessary for the Officer walking the beat to use the call box, which was hardwired to a switch board at the police station that was manned by an operator twenty-four hours a day.

If the operator didn't talk to the beat officer

every hour on the hour of the day the police department would send a zone car out to find the beat officer for his safety.

Throughout the city there were several walking beats: two downtown, two in Ybor City, and one in West Tampa.

In recent years, 2019 or so, I became the proud owner of the call box that was situated at the corner of 16th Street and 7th Avenue That call box is attached to my home in the pool area and it has displayed inside it the names of several officers who walked that beat, including my own.

Dry Humor

One of the downtown beats was located on Franklin Street in the business district of downtown Tampa. This beat was a step up from the one on skid row. The officers assigned to any of the beats had the ability to walk from one to another although it was frowned upon by the Supervisors.

The downtown beat was usually manned by a police officer named "Vern." He was a peculiar chap who had a weird sense of humor.

One such instance reflecting his odd sense was when this officer was standing in front of a bank one day. He was approached by a lady and her young son. She inquired of the officer the location of the very bank he was in front of.

The policeman asked the lady and her son, "Would you please follow me?"

The officer then crossed the street with them in tow and walked to the middle of the block across from where he was originally turned and pointed his finger at the bank and told the lady. "There it is ma'am."

The lady failed to see the humor of this police officer and called her husband to report this mishap; her husband was Chief Mullins, the chief of the Tampa Police Department! Uh oh!!!

(Once you were a police officer for three years, you no longer were considered a rookie. You could then be assigned to different squads with different sergeants and even different sections of the city.

This part of the writing will deal with several of these assignments so it will jump back and forth as my career jumped all over the place.)

Sergeant Jim Mishak

I was fortunate to have developed many close friendships which served me well during my thirteen and one half years before my career ended as a result of a ninety-five mile an hour day time auto accident at Palm Avenue and 11th Street on a lazy Sunday afternoon.

My first Sergeant, as I recall, was Sergeant Jim Mishak. He was a calm, well thought of, easy going individual who watched over his squad as if we were all his kids. In this Sergeant's eyes we could do no wrong. He was proud of his squad.

At this point of the story it is necessary to explain that the city was divided in half, basically by the Hillsborough River. The type of police service rendered differed, depending upon which side of the river you lived on.

Things that were done in District Two on the east side of town just wouldn't fly in District One on the west side of town. It's sad to say, but that was the way it was back then.

One Sunday our Sergeant summoned my partner and me to his home. Upon arrival, we found that he and his wife were sitting poolside. The Sergeant told his wife to go to the bar and get two Tom Collins drinks, one for each of us. When we questioned his offer, his response was, "I'm your boss aren't I? Drink up."

TGH

During the assignment with Sergeant Mishak, I was assigned several times to Tampa General Hospital. It was there that I made great friends with the nurses and Doctors who worked there at that time.

What better friends could a cop have? These were friends who could someday help save your life.

Needless to say, those nurses and Doctors possessed "*get out of jail free cards*" for the most part. I was an *active, hands on* cop. I made several trips for lacerations, broken noses and such. They were always there for me, ready to help.

I recall a crazy incident that occurred one night on the midnight shift. After pulling up to the ER and getting out of my patrol car, an escapee from the nut ward, dressed only in a hospital gown, ran across the parking lot and jumped headfirst into the Seddon Channel behind the hospital.

The nurses asked me to save this poor soul. Not being a good swimmer, I refused. I would have only made this bad situation worse.

While I was trying to think of a different way to help, a supervisor named *Jack Johnson* drove up. Not thinking twice, he took off his gun belt and shoes. He tied a rope around his upper body, handed me the other end of the rope, and jumped in. He grabbed the escapee and told me to pull them both toward the sea wall.

And pull them I did!

He never let me forget the rope burn I caused him during that incident.

Jack was a very special person. He loved to call me by my nickname "The Guinea", which I received because of my Sicilian descent.

That nickname stuck with me throughout my career. I didn't take offense at that name then, or now.

That reference would get you fired nowadays.

Sergeant Johnson's aunt was the charge nurse in the ER on the midnight shift along with "Kelly", a sweet good looking red head that we all loved.

Kelly in later life became an alcoholic but continued to work in the ER. Just before she retired, several other officers and I would station ourselves along the route she traveled to work.

We made sure she made it to work, safe and sound.

II

Who's Who

In my thirteen and one half years of my being a police officer, many circumstances occurred which had positive effects on my life and family. In this writing, I may inadvertently omit or unknowingly misreport an incident. Let it be known that any and all incidents related in this writing are correct to the best of my recollection.

There are so many stories to tell and so many interesting people who make up this writing. Just by volume alone, incidents are bound to be slightly misreported or inadvertently omitted. I beg your forgiveness in advance for any and all shortcomings.

Roll Call

Let me name at this point as many of my supervisors as I can remember:

- Sergeant Jim Mishak
- Sergeant Frank B. Woodlee
- Sergeant Roy Sharpless
- Sergeant Jake Mason
- Sergeant Jerry Godwin
- Sergeant Dick Cowan
- Sergeant John Francis Brannigan
- Sergeant H. B. Maxey
- Sergeant Justo Cohalla

All of the above supervisors were excellent police officers and they all had their own way of doing things. This made working under them very interesting.

For the most part, I worked well with them all. I gave them my loyalty and friendship while working for them.

Sergeant Frank Byrd Woodlee

In life we all have people in our lives that we gravitate to more than others. Early on in my career I became very close to my second Sergeant Frank Byrd Woodlee.

Sergeant Woodlee assumed command over Sergeant Jim Mishak's squad when Jim retired.

Frank walked into his first roll call and informed us the assignments would remain unchanged. At this point I had been walking the beat in Ybor City for three months.

About two months after Frank took over he pulled up to me while I was walking the beat on the evening shift. He motioned for me to get in the car with him.

Once inside he asked me, "You've been walking this beat for about five months, correct?"

I answered him, "Yes, Sergeant, about that length of time."

His next question and my answer to it was the beginning of a lifelong friendship which I cherish to this day. He asked me: "Would you rather work for me?"

You can easily guess what my answer was!

If Frank Woodlee liked you, you had a guardian angel from that time forward.

Let me share an example here.

I would be working for another squad and he would see a better opportunity for me. He would then call me and ask how I was doing and did I like the Sergeant I was working for. No matter what my answer was, his next question always was, "Would you rather work for me?"

After my answer he would say to me, "Report to my roll call tonight. You have been transferred to my squad." He would then add, "The chief has already approved the move."

Sergeant Woodlee helped command a unit within the Tampa Police Department known as the Selective Enforcement Unit or SEU. This unit consisted of approximately forty members, which included three sergeants. The unit worked at the pleasure of the Mayor of the city of Tampa under the direct orders of the Chief of Police. We worked parades, burglary saturation, robbery stakeouts, and drug trafficking – *just about anything thinkable or unthinkable.*

Here's a cute story of how this unit worked.

Sergeant Woodlee came to roll call one evening on the midnight shift. He ordered each of us to come to roll call the next night with a new tool in our arsenal in which to fight crime – *an ice pick!*

The next evening we were given our assignments for that night but only after showing him that we all had our new tool.

What were those assignments?

He said to us, "You guys are going to work the Six Mile Creek area this evening. You all know who the bad guys are and where they live, correct?"

Six Mile Creek was *not* a good area. It was filled with an abundance of lowlife individuals.

After receiving an affirmative response from us to that question, he said in a convincing voice, "Go find their cars and flatten all four of their tires with those ice picks. Make sure to ice pick the tire stems. Let's see if they are willing to walk to their next crime scene."

Our targets were not productive at all that day.

This great man watched over me and my family, including my wife and children, until God made our friendship end when he called Frank home.

I was a pall bearer at his service.

Major Vance Fairbanks

While speaking of great Police Officers, I would be remiss if I didn't mention another one

of my mentors and guardian angels, Major
Vance Fairbanks.

The Fairbanks family had a lock on the
Tampa Police Department. All four brothers
were sworn police officers at the same time.
They were Vance, Johnny, Gary, and Billy.

Vance was fond of me, I think, because his
favorite son and I shared our first name, "Joey".
Vance left this earth as the result of an accident.
And yes, as you might guess, I forced my way
into being a pall bearer for Vance as well. It was
only appropriate that I help carry a man to his
final resting place who had carried me during
my time as a police officer.

May both of these great men be remembered
and allowed to *rest in peace.*

Bill Driggers

When you worked for Frank Woodlee and
Vance Fairbanks, you knew they had your back.
I love to tell anyone who will listen that the
popular TV series, Chicago PD, was written with
Frank in mind. The character *Sergeant Hank
Voigt* was Frank Woodlee incarnate.

One evening shift, just prior to the Super
Bowl in Tampa, I was partnered up with Officer
Gary Fairbanks (Vance's Brother). As we were

leaving the station, Officer Bill Driggers, one of our own unit, was attempting to get the entire SEU unit to call in sick on Super Bowl Sunday. He even named it the *Blue Flu.*

Hearing this, I confronted this officer. I assured him that I was going to return to the office and tell then Captain Woodlee the dastardly deed he was attempting. I assured him that it was I that was going to report this incident now.

Upon my informing Captain Woodlee, Driggers was immediately confronted. He was given the opportunity to resign or, in case he refused, he would be terminated on the spot.

Driggers resigned. He had not honored the words "total loyalty."

More SEU

Officer Jim Harris, myself and two other police officers, (one nicknamed "Hawk"), were attempting to make some drug buys in the area of Lake Avenue near Central in an area known as "Robles Park."

The four of us ended up in a neighborhood bar drinking beer and playing pool. I engaged a patron in a game of pool, which ended up being several pool games for money.

I was three hundred dollars up on this guy when he announced that he didn't have any money. While trying to figure out what we were going to do about this welcher, we heard sirens and they were getting closer.

We soon discovered that "Hawk" wasn't anywhere to be seen. The last time we saw him, he was drunk.

As uniformed police officers were arriving at the scene, "Hawk" dropped out of a tree, and started running away.

It was pretty obvious from their behavior that the uniformed police officers were going to shoot him.

We all quickly, and in unison, identified ourselves. Fortunately, all went well. We even found Hawk several hours later.

We found out the he had shinnied up the tree & was peeking into the bedroom of a married couple.

Clearly it was a peeping Tom, or rather, a Peeping Hawk!

Sergeant Cohalla's Squad

The following is about evening shift in Ybor City where Sergeant Justo Cohalla, Officer Bill

Brown, and I are the main characters in the story.

I would like to start the story off by saying that I was walking the beat. In truth, I was actually watching a porn movie on the screen in the Ritz Theater

While I was clearly minding my own business, I was most rudely interrupted by the non-English speaking establishment's manager.

He was saying something in Spanish which I was able to roughly translate to, "Police man! Hurry up! There are two black men breaking into a clothing store."

I was on the move!

I sped past the popcorn machine. (This was the very machine I would eventually nickname Officer Pete Saunders after. I'll share more about that amusing incident later.) I had a walkie-talkie in my left hand and was calling for help. I had my thirty-eight service revolver in my right hand.

As I ran towards 16th Street and 7th Avenue, I observed several older Latin men sitting on a short wall engaged in checker games with one another.

Beyond them is where I saw two young black males taking clothing out of the display window. The window in question was part of the Rainbow

Clothing Store. It was owned by a couple I've known since I was a teenager – a Mr. & Mrs. Verkauf.

The black males had mannequins with clothing on them. Because of constant sun exposure, the clothing on the mannequins was sun rotted and fell apart when touched. They really wouldn't get any value from these stiffs.

But they were thieves, or at least vandals, and they were committing a crime.

As I was readying my aim to shoot at the pair, I noted that if I missed I would shoot out the large window of the Cannon Shoe Store owned by Mr. Frank Adamo.

I held my fire. I would never hear the end of that story if that occurred.

When I arrived at 7th Avenue and 16th Street. I could see clearly to Adamo Drive. I yelled, "Drop those clothes or I will shoot you."

The guy threw the rotten clothes down on the sidewalk. I took one shot at him anyway. He turned right into an alley and he disappeared.

That is, all except for a little blood that he left behind as a gift of sorts.

The second suspect ran to about 5th Avenue where this guy, named Roundtree, engaged Officer W.D. Brown in a fight. While running east from that location, Officer Brown had unloaded six shots from his service revolver at the fleeing felon.

The fleeing suspect was eventually apprehended by another member of our squad.

Officer Brown reported to Sergeant Cohalla that he saw all six of the bullets that he fired leave the barrel of his gun, travel about ten feet, and fall to the sidewalk and street in front of him.

Brown was insistent that the ammunition had failed. Giving him every benefit of a doubt, our squad decided that we were going to help him find those bullets.

We lined up three or four squad cars and pointed them at the area in question.

Hell! Were we ever surprised!

With the aid of their headlights, we actually found all six of those bullets, right exactly where Brown said they would be found.

The next morning Major Morton heard about the crappy ammo story. He summoned me into his office.

Let me interject something here. So you know where he and I stood, Major Sid Morton and I were pretty close. We talked pretty plainly to each other.

Morton asked me if my bullet firing efforts resulted in failure as well.

I assured him that I would never rely on that crappy city issued ammo. I confided in him that my ammo was loaded by a fireman friend of mine and it was special. I told him that the first round I fire is to illuminate the area.

That afternoon all our department ammo was replaced.

The next morning, our squad did a *double back*. That term means that we got off at eleven at night and returned to the day shift at seven-thirty in the morning.

About nine o'clock, a black male with two black females had robbed a Save-Rite grocery store located on Nebraska, North of MLK Boulevard.

A helicopter was used to search the area and it found the car that was used. It was still in transit.

The chopper followed the suspect's car to the jail on Morgan Street. We found out later that this is where the black male driver was going to use the ill-gained cash to bond out Mr. Roundtree from a few hours earlier.

Detectives noticed that the bad guy had an Ace bandage on his right arm to cover up some blood leakage.

After quite a few questions, the suspect finally told the investigating detectives that he had received the gunshot wound while breaking into the Rainbow Clothing Store.

He also protested and said that he didn't think I should have shot him.

He said that he had complied with my order to drop the clothes and was cooperating.

Poor baby.

My Missing Badge

While working for Sergeant Justo Cohalla on an evening shift, I somehow managed to lose my badge off my uniform shirt.

Trying not to put Justo in the situation of having to write me up for losing city equipment (the badge), I wore my jacket to conceal the fact that my badge was missing.

This purposeful deception on my part continued successfully for about two weeks.

As luck would have it, I eventually got a phone call from the Florida Highway Patrol Office. It was the one located on East Hillsborough Avenue and 30th Street.

The duty officer asked me if he was addressing Corporal Severino and if my badge number was 468.

After answering "yes" to both questions, he informed me that he had my badge in his hand.

I thought myself, "Yay!"

It seems that someone was driving on Hillsborough Avenue and hit the badge. I guess it was likely in the gutter by then.

The driver stopped to see what glittery object he had run over. Once he discovered what it was, he turned it into the patrol station.

Sergeant Cohalla was never the wiser.

Major Earl Hainey (SEU)

I'm not sure if this big ole cracker liked me or not. However, I think that he liked me, because every time an assignment would come up that was new he seemed to give me the right of first refusal.

This occurred for assignments such as the Salt & Pepper team for the Central Avenue beat and the first Police observer program. For example, both Joe Joeb and I were offered the assignment first. I accepted every opportunity I was offered.

The police observer program was interesting. It was a twenty-eight day assignment that consisted of riding in a police helicopter. The observer's job was to stay in contact with the officers on the ground. When needed, we would direct the pilot as to what support was required. This freed up the pilot to fly the craft much more safely.

This assignment came with its own set of unique circumstances. The pilots were two recently discharged Cobra gunship pilots from the US Army. Both were nice guys and incredibly competent helicopter pilots.

The 'copters were stored at Peter O'Knight Airport on Davis Island. On the first night of the twenty-eight days, the pilot put me in the second seat and buckled me into it. He then instructed me on how to operate the intercom system. It consisted of two switches mounted on the floor of the copter. The one on the left was to access communication with the pilot only. The one on the right was activated to converse only with

KIB459, radio. If you toggled both of them, everyone could hear the conversation.

I asked him, "How fast would the ship take off?"

He thought I had said that I was ready to go, and off we went.

The force sent me forward and I inadvertently toggled both switches and responded vocally something like: "Holy Shit."

With that communication, the dispatcher, knowing it was a mistake, responded, "KIB459, unit ten-nine that last transmission."

Ten-nine means, "Please repeat your last transmission."

I didn't.

The pilot, prior to the last flight of the night, took the craft to approx 4500 feet over Peter O'Knight airport.

It suddenly became very still and extremely quiet. When I inquired as to the cause, I was told the pilot turned the damn engine off and we were free falling out of the night sky.

Well, I told him in no uncertain terms to *turn the damn thing back on.* I remember that I was quite insistent in this!

I was told that it's called "auto-rotation" and it's a common maneuver; at least for the pilot.

As for me, I give absolutely no thanks to him for the missing heads up.

Damn Hotshot!

Joe Saenz

Let's keep the helicopter stories together!

I'm going to jump ahead to after I retired.

I was working as a 911 Supervisor. I got a call from my dear friend, Joe Saenz, who had become a senior pilot.

The night that he retired, he called me at the 911 radio room and asked me to come out to the airport for a nice 'copter ride.

I said, "Sure!" Then I advised my friend that I needed to first get the proper papers together to legally take the offered ride.

Joe replied to me, "Don't bother! If we crash and die... what are they going to do? Fire us? Forget that nonsense! Come on out here!"

He made sense. So out I went, and wow! Did I get a Star Wars ride of a lifetime!

And no one but us knew about it, until now.

MD 20/20

Now that I've just shared a story about Joe Saenz, the largest Mexican I have ever met, here's a story I know he will remember.

Joe and Doug Paisley were the best of friends and were in the SEU. One time we got an assignment to stop robberies occurring near the local Tampa train station. We got together and planned our approach. Once we all agreed, we went to the Army Navy Store on Florida Avenue to purchase what would easily be thought of as a bum's costume.

Once purchased, we went to town on Joe to make him appear like a local street bum.

We put dirt on his face and placed a bottle of MD 20/20 in his coat pocket, with it sticking out like a red flag.

We sent Joe off to start his roaming.

Unfortunately, this was premature.

Before we could set up to watch out for him, we heard two or three gun shots being fired from Joe's direction.

When we got there to see what had occurred, we found that three black males had knocked Joe on the head with the very wine bottle we put into his pocket!

One of them had straddled a dazed Joe and was going thru his coat pockets.

While all this was going on, Joe regained his senses and interrupted the thief.

How?

He first interrupted him by the sound of a chief special's hammer being cocked. Then he really interrupted the thief when the big Mexican shot him in the forehead.

Suffice it to say that the criminal quite literally *lost his mind.*

❧------❦

Robert Price

Here's another story related to my days in the SEU. Like I said before, I couldn't make up this stuff. Yet, it's all true.

Something occurred. There was a campaign started by someone in the chain of command. Ultimately, the job of making sure that campaign was fulfilled was given to the SEU.

I know the answer as to why. But, I won't knowingly disclose the reason here; at least, not directly.

Our part of this campaign started off by our Major and Captain explaining the desired result they were looking to obtain. They told the forty of us, all working the midnight shift (eleven am to seven am), that for the next month they wanted to "Put assholes on the peg." They then explained, "This is the peg, and we want to put assholes on it."

Let me more clearly explain this. They wanted for us to put multiple charges upon anyone we legitimately arrested. For example, when you stop someone for speeding and their license was expired, we were to charge them for both offenses – no exceptions.

We were to start immediately!

So, that night I drove out onto my beat, with my marching orders in hand.

As I was coming out of Drew Park that first night, I stopped a car around Dale Mabry and Osborne. The driver was one Robert Price. He was approximately twenty-one years of age. Robert was recently discharged from the military. I think it might have been from the Air Force.

Unfortunately for Mr. Price, he had two underage girls in his vehicle with him. In addition to this, all three of them had open containers of beer in their possession.

Robert pleaded with me to not take any actions that would negatively impact his future. He added that he was supposed to be interviewed the following Monday morning. *That interview was for being hired as a Tampa Police Officer.*

Here's where you may not agree with my decision.

I arrested everyone. I put several "assholes" on the peg from that one stop.

As fate would have it, Mr. Price was hired by the Tampa PD. He eventually made it to the rank of Captain as well. I even watched and assisted him later in life in becoming a Master Mason.

And the greatest aspect of this is that there were absolutely no hard feelings on either side.

He obviously got his act together, and then some!

Getting Legal

One night I was walking through the halls of 1710 Tampa Street on the way to an evening shift. On my way to shift, I was advised by my sergeant not to carry the illegal gun I had in my possession.

He also told me that if I needed that type of weapon I should secure one from our police armory.

Being a reasonable person, the next night I followed his advice.

At approximately two am, I was traveling on Kennedy Boulevard eastbound at MacDill in a unmarked car. A driver going the other direction in a very reckless manner attracted my attention.

I gave him pursuit. Only problem was that the more I pursued him, the more reckless he became.

I had already made up my mind that this jerk was going to spend the night at the Gray Bar Motel a.k.a. the County Jail.

I finally got him to stop on Dale Mabry in front of the well-known "Space Ship."

I arrested him without hesitation.

It should have been an easy and uncomplicated night, but things were panning out differently for me.

While waiting for a wrecker and Paddy Wagon, I observed an assault involving gunfire. The assailant then turned his anger toward me.

Needless to say, this was the biggest mistake of his life. He had brought a puny pistol to a well-stocked shotgun fight.

My supervisor soon arrived to the scene. He was kind of surprised that I had followed his advice from the night before. This was the advice that involved the illegal shotgun that I had been riding with.

The rest of this story will not be shared in these pages. I will tell you that it all ended well.

High Placed Friends

At one point, I decided to take the Sergeant's Promotional exam (passing this exam was a prerequisite for promotion to any rank, not just Sergeant). Being a pretty good speller, I whizzed through the spelling portion of the exam.

After returning home I was asked by my spouse how I thought I fared. I told her that out of the one hundred or so words on the spelling portion there were two words that I struggled with.

She asked me which were the words and I asked, (I badly garbling the pronunciation), "What the hell is a *Chihuahua*?"

She answered, "That's a small short-haired Mexican dog."

The other word was *chicanery*.

She responded to that word with, "It's when you attempt to fool someone."

Oh well! I passed anyway!

I went back to my squad and continued what I had been doing for the past several years, breaking in new police officers.

After getting off one morning at 7 am, I went upstairs and knocked on my friend Major Vance Fairbanks' office door.

He asked, "Who is it?"

I responded, "The Guinea!"

I was invited into his office and was pleasantly surprised.

He was having a bullshitting session with my other mentor, Captain Frank Woodlee.

He asked how he could help me.

I asked him to tell my Major in District Two, that I was on the Sergeant's Promotion list, that there was a Corporal slot open, and that since I was on the Sergeant's list after passing the exam I was now qualified for Corporal and that he should promote me to that position.

Major Fairbanks looked at me and asked, "You want me to tell Major Briggs that he should promote you?"

I said, "Yes, please, and thank you."

I then exited the office, went home, took a shower, blacked out the room, and went to bed for some much needed rest.

Forgetting all about my request, I heard my wife explaining to someone in the next room that she wasn't going to wake me up.

I asked her who was on the phone.

She said, "Major Clayton Briggs."

I picked up the phone and asked him what he needed.

He informed me that he had just promoted me to the rank of Corporal and he advised me not to disappoint him.

I assured him he made a good decision.

I guess the squeaky wheel gets the grease.

The promotion gave me the feeling that I had finally accomplished something worthwhile in my career.

From that day forward my career felt more rewarding. Being able to interact as the second in charge of a patrol squad brought me great personal satisfaction.

Now come some stories about the eight or nine months of my career that were most especially fun.

This assignment was expected and I think was offered to me because of the pronunciation of my last name. I was assigned to the Vice Squad supervised by Captain Warren Lawson, Sergeant Mario Sanez (The Hatchet Man), Sergeant Donald Newberger of the Newberger fame. (The Newbergers have been involved in law enforcement forever.) There were even three women on the squad at that time - Myrt Ellis, Patricia Pierce, and a pretty blonde named Barbara Cueto.

I believe the *powers that be* thought I should be on the team because of my surname. They wrongly assumed that I was a numbers expert!

I really wouldn't have known a Bolita[1] ticket from a grapefruit.

I survived eight to nine months thanks to my partner Louie Cueto and the famous "Bo" Woolweaver.

---

[1] a game of chance having the character of a lottery in which a bag of small numbered balls is tossed about until only one remains or until one is grasped at random, the ball so selected being considered as bearing the winning number.

Popcorn Pete

I have a great story about a stocky, no neck cracker boy who wore western shirts and jeans and could ride a Harley standing on the seat on a sea wall. He could also hand you your head if he chose to.

This fellow's name was "Pete" and I may as well tell his story now.

Pete was a very nice man whose expertise was riding motorcycles. He, along with his friend Russell Groover, were responsible for teaching cops to ride.

Pete, when either mad or excited, had a tendency to stutter a little. Well, one night Pete and I decided that we would go to the dog track and see what we could see. The track was closed when we got there because President Eisenhower had just passed away and all federal related organizations were shut down.

With it being shut down, Pete said to me, "Now what do we do?"

I replied, "Hey, Pete! Why don't we go catch some homosexuals?"

Yes. Things were obviously different back then.

Pete responded, "Do you know how?"

I answered, "No, but I'll bet we can figure it out."

Pete agreed and off to the Ritch Theater we went, holding hands, skipping, and singing "Kumbaya!"

When we arrived, I stayed in the lobby watching some really bad old porn on their movie screen. I watched Pete go into the main seating area of the theater. Pete soon came out and headed for the rest room, wringing his hands together and stuttering and cursing at the same time.

Thinking he was going to choke someone, I followed.

Inside the restroom was only Pete and myself and he wouldn't tell me why he was so pissed off. I followed him back into the theater. He soon emerged with a skinny white guy. It seems this guy had asked Pete if he wanted some popcorn, pointing to the bag on his lap. Unknown to Pete, the guy had unzipped his zipper, torn a hole in the bottom of the bag and inserted something through it. When Pete reached into the bag to grab a handful of popcorn, what he grabbed was most definitely *not* popcorn!

In that moment, I nicknamed him "Popcorn Pete" and called him that from that day forward.

Luis Cueto and I were partnered up as a Bolita team. We did a lot of entertaining in the bars in Tampa attempting to make Bolita cases.

My cousins owned one of the lounges on Kennedy named the Chez Louie, which was a classy night club.

One night, while in my cousins' club, the famous drummer Gene Krupa was on stage. He was beating up a drum set while toking on a joint in plain sight. Someone wanted to arrest the entertainer and my cousins, who owned the club, said, "Don't go there!"

Needless to say, *that dog didn't hunt that night*.

Once my secret was out in the open that I wasn't a Bolita expert as it had been assumed I was, that I was just another pretty face in a five hundred dollar Botany Five Hundred Suit, back to patrol I went.

Truthfully, it was exactly where I belonged.

Pete Saunders' Motorcycle Guru

Let me share a little bit more here about Popcorn. Pete was the department's motorcycle instructor along with Officer Russell Groover.

Tampa was broken down into seventeen patrol zones. The call names we used for these zones were *Zone One, Zone Two*, and so on.

We also had names for our specialty units. They were identified as *Motor One, Motor Two,* and so on.

Officer Pete Saunders was always Motor One if he was riding his motorcycle.

As soon as Officer Saunders keyed his microphone and spoke, you knew Popcorn Pete was on air; especially if he was stuttering.

One night Motor One keyed his microphone and told the dispatcher that he was on the Gandy Bridge attempting to stop a vehicle.

The dispatcher immediately cleared the radio by announcing "All units standby, Motor One has the air."

She continued to interact with Pete as we were all hauling our butts over toward his location to help, aid, and assist excitable Pete.

As we traveled in his direction, the next and very last transmission we heard from Motor One

 was that he was in a high speed pursuit at ninety miles per hour and that he was in a

49

high speed waggle.

From that point on, all we heard was dead air. There were no more words from Motor One to be heard.

When backup arrived at the scene, they found out why. Pete had been forced to lay down that big ol' hog of his on the bridge. As he did, he stood up on that bike's gas tank, used the right handle to guide the Harley, and rode that hog out like that till it came to a full stop.

When we came upon the scene, we saw the extremely long skid mark his hog had made. It told us that Pete had ridden Motor One like a skateboard for quite a stretch.

Fortunately for our Popcorn Pete, he escaped without a scratch.

Do You Know about Bolita?

For about two to three weeks I hung around Ybor City following a Latin male suspected as a Bolita peddler. This fellow's name was "Max."

He never knew I was trailing him until a Saturday morning. It was at the Cuban club and it was at about ten or eleven in the morning.

I was sitting in the main part of the first floor of the Cuban club. I was doing so in plain sight of the bar and the two cash registers on the back-bar. I was also accompanied by several non-Spanish speaking police officers.

On the Saturday in question an elderly Latin man was behind the bar. This older man's name was "un oyeido." This translates to "one ear".

There was a pay phone on the wall of the club. It was the type that could only receive incoming calls. The phone rang. Someone answered and announced, "Max, telefino! Max, the phone's for you!"

Max came up, answered the phone, and wrote down a series of numbers in a small note book.

This occurred many more times that morning. Max continued coming to the phone and writing in his little book.

Finally, Max went to the bar and handed the one eared older man the paper he had written on.

The old man took the paper and placed it into one of the cash registers.

The older man announced that he was leaving and was headed out the door. The warrant was only good on the premises of the Cuban club so the old man unknowingly forced my hand. Timing was essential and, in the case, everything!

I quickly yelled from across the room, "Grab him before he gets out!"

With that, a police officer grabbed the old man.

Unfortunately, the timing was not so good. The one eared old man clutched his chest and proceeded to have a heart attack.

Fire Rescue was summoned but the Cubans present wanted to physically carry him to the Tries Clinic about three blocks away.

Out of respect for the old man, I allowed it.

Once things quieted down, I left with Max under arrest. The one eared old man was on his way to the ER at Tampa General.

On my way out, I spied the father of a friend of mine sitting at a table. I foolishly approached him, spoke momentarily with him, and then left.

By the time I got home, my phone was ringing off the hook.

You guessed it! It was the guy I foolishly approached before leaving. He was screaming at me in Spanish, "Damn Joe! Now they think I set the arrest up! They think I'm a ratone[2]!"

More Bolita

If it is not clear by now, let me stress strongly

---

[2] a rat

that Tampa was a home to the illegal lottery *Bolita* that originated Cuba.

Several different elements controlled the sale and distribution of this game. Generally, the numbers played by the public were written in one form or another day to day until the daily results were known. This was a daily activity and had some real characters involved.

One evening, while checking in on one of the most well-known Bolita peddlers, I entered a small grocery store that he was running on Nebraska Avenue. It was close to the downtown train station. The operator of the illegal lottery was manning the grocery store himself. He had another person with him as well.

After I greeted this elderly man and his companion, he asked me, "How have you been? Was there anything I could do to help you?"

Knowing the answer I would have been given, I told him, "I wanted to purchase those three cans of green beans that are on the shelf behind the register."

He told me, "You really don't want them."

After I insisted, I found out why he was reluctant to make the sale. *All three cans were empty!* The green beans were already consumed. The cans were just a front for his lottery operation.

Needless to say, there were no beans to sell. So I left, having made my presence in the neighborhood known to him.

When I got back into my unmarked car and began to leave the area, the man's accomplice walked out to my car and placed a fifth of a scotch in a brown paper bag on my rear floor board. Apparently, this lottery owner knew he could have had a major hassle with me, and

wanted to let me know he appreciated me treating him easy.

Knowing that this gift could have been construed to be a bribe, I drove directly to the station and asked Mike Cather what I should do with this gift.

Mike said to me, "If you don't drink it, I will."

My problem was solved.

District Two

Once back to where I belonged in District Two as a Corporal, my career continued along its meager path.

After an unfortunate car crash which eventually forced me into retirement, I had several assignments involving many different supervisors. Funny thing is, I usually ending up right back with my favorite supervisor, Frank B. Woodlee.

While doing several stints in SEU, the basic rules remained the same. One of the rules was that if you ever were involved in a situation where you have to shoot and kill someone, we were to call another SEU unit to the scene immediately. We were to make sure our stories matched and then call Capt. Woodlee. He would handle it from there.

I bring this up because something bad occurred while attempting to pay an informant for some information that we just received. We were in an unmarked car in Port Tampa and the driver was Sleepy Eyed Jim. As we drove around the area, a group of young men were following us.

Officer Jim Harris suggested to me that they were going to throw rocks at us. He then said to me that if that started, I should call 10-24 because he was going to shoot at them.

The adrenaline and the testosterone level were high. As suggested, they did indeed throw rocks at us and Jim shot at them in return.

I called 10-24.

After the mini riot, Capt Woodlee addressed the 10-24 call. He asked me if I was bleeding or was I really in danger.

I tried to lay the blame on Harris.

Well, the wily old Capt Woodlee saw through that crap. Being my friend, he gently read me the riot act and then asked me, "If Harris asked you to jump off a bridge, would you?"

That was Captain Woodlee's way of handling things. Once he addressed an issue, he didn't harp on the same issue again. He moved on.

Captain Woodlee soon assigned me a task which involved the use of the old bread truck with Georgia plates and running boards. I was tasked with picking someone from our ranks that I trusted for this dastardly deed I was going to accomplish.

I chose a member to help me.

The assignment was to park across from a Firestone tire shop located on 22nd Street one block south of Hillsborough Avenue. There was intelligence that a recently paroled prisoner was going to break into that store, as he used to work there. The suspect was going to steal their truck. He was to use a twenty-two caliber pistol, drive the truck thru the service doors, and then flee.

I was asked to end this fellow's criminal career, if it were possible. I was also told to use a twelve gauge pump shotgun, if necessary.

On the way to the stake out my partner asked me to stop at a 7-Eleven as he was thirsty. I complied. When we set up on the scene, I heard the sound of what I thought was a can of coke. I found out that it was really a can of Miller High Life beer.

While waiting patiently for things to unfold, my beeper sounded off. It was a personal call I had been hoping for. I then drove the bread truck to the nearest pay phone booth, which was about a block away, out of sight of the tire store.

If you haven't guessed by now, the suspect did exactly what we were told he would do, but without us there.

A uniformed police officer named Bobby Jordan confronted the suspect at the scene with no foreknowledge of our orders.

He engaged him in a gun fight and killed the suspect. This was a surprising outcome, because Officer Jordan was not a very good marksman.

You can only imagine what my friend Captain Woodlee had to say to me about my indiscretion in abandoning my station to take a personal call. That was the maddest he had ever been at me and rightly so.

He advised me that if we hadn't had the past we shared he would have sent me by the way of Officer Bill Driggers! (Do you remember that earlier "Blue Flu" Incident?)

It was a close call and another example of how we looked out for each other.

Major Vance Fairbanks and Capt Woodlee often rode together for company. There was a series of armed robberies in Tampa. They were done by a commuter bus guy who would cover his face with Band-Aids. He used them as his mask. He was therefore dubbed the Band Aid Bandit.

At one point, the Major and the Captain decided that they would try and help us apprehend this culprit. One day soon after they made their decision, they parked across the street from a possible target.

Much to their surprise, they were told afterward that they unknowingly observed the suspect commit the very robbery that they were there to catch him doing.

It is just as well. Half the time neither of these two fine police officers carried a weapon!

The Florida State Fair

As mentioned before the SEU unit was involved in multiple scenarios. One of them was working the Florida State Fair every year. The fair was a fifteen day assignment with no days off and the work was usually done in full uniform.

The fair at that time was located on North Boulevard between Cass Street and North B Street. This encompassed the campus of the University of Tampa. The midway was under the control of an older Carney named "Whitey Wise." This was his nickname because of his looks.

Whitey's word was Gospel and law. Because of the nature of the carnival, sometimes law enforcement and carnies didn't mix well.

One season there was a booth on the midway whose owners didn't like our presence, so every time we'd walk by their booth they would make duck and pig sounds.

After learning of this inappropriate conduct Whitey took it upon himself to take retribution against these clowns. He threw them off the midway during a violent thunderstorm. This most probably ruined their equipment.

Police officers were ordered not to participate in any games of chance during their time working the fair. A Carney, knowing that my wife had just delivered my first son, Michael, wanted him to have an extra-large stuffed animal. I soon came into our makeshift office under the bleachers carrying a giant stuffed toy which we were not allowed to accept.

I caught all kinds of crap over that one.

At that same fair, some kids from the neighborhood were throwing pieces of granite from a nearby railroad track over the fence and into the fair grounds. They were injuring the fair's patrons.

SEU went to the rescue.

What was our solution?

We went to the affected area and threw rocks back at the suspects.

We won!

They were dispatched by David. The Philistines were defeated!

Some Fair Background

While on the subject of the State Fair, I need to give you some of the back story on my experiences with the State Fair earlier in my life..

My father Amato Severino worked for and became Salvatore "RED" Italiano's assistant. Red was the owner of Anthony Distributors, a Miller High Life beer distributor located on Grand Central Avenue and Rome.

Red's son Tony Italiano took over the day to day operation of three beer distributorships: Tampa, Pinellas Beer & Wine, and Holiday Distributorship in Holiday Florida.

Uncle Tony had two sons, Salvatore and Anthony ,who were both my age, and he also had a step son our age named Mark. They were both unofficially my "cousins".[3]

Being young, we desired to attend the Fair every year. The Italiano family by no stretch of the imagination needed any financial assistance.

During the fair, Uncle Tony would invite me to tag along. This was because of my father. Upon arrival at the fairgrounds, Uncle Tony would go and see Mr. Carl Saddlemyer.

Carl was the CEO of the Royal American Shows. He controlled the Fair and all its parts.

Mr. Saddlemyer would take a particular ring from his pinky finger and give it to my Uncle Tony. Uncle Tony would wear this ring which allowed him and his guests total and complete

---

[3] Cousins by association not by blood

access to the entire Fair, including shows, rides, and games, and even food as well.

All was provided without question. This was the magic of this ring.

Uncle Pat

My father and mother became great friends with Pat & Leigh Sirignano. They were more like an Aunt & Uncle to me (in the "by association" category rather than actual blood). We spent many Christmas Eves at my Uncle Pat's house, which was located near the river.

Aunt Leigh had a brother who was a Carney for the Royal American Shows. Her brother's show name was *Tony Paradise*. He was a side show geek before he joined Harlem in Havana as a Barker. Harlem in Havana was a girlie show.

So there's no confusion in my story, I'm now returning to the time of being an adult Tampa Police Officer.

One Christmas Eve while at Uncle Pat's house, Tony Paradise asked me to bring him a Pilsner beer glass and three new Gillette blue blades from Uncle Pat's shaving kit. He told me to get the blades that were new and not used.

When I complied with his request he proceeded to eat the three razor blades and the beer glass.

To my amazement he didn't die.

During that same night an older lady showed up for dinner. She was introduced to me as *Dolly Madison*. She was employed by the Royal American Shows as well.

Dolly didn't eat glass. Her job was even more essential. Dolly was a *Fixer* for the Royal American Shows. Dolly traveled to the next venue ahead of the show. Her job was to identify and to grease the palms of those that were responsible for allowing the show to go on or disallowing it!!

Gasparilla Jail

This included County Commissioners, City Councilmen, and anyone else who could be bribed to allow the uninterrupted circus to continue. *The fair must go on!*

During Gasparilla Day one year the Grand Marshall was an older appellate Judge from Orlando Florida. The pirates were getting arrested by the handful.

Most Gasparilla pirates are professionals. They are Doctors, lawyers, and Indian chiefs.

Our makeshift jail at that event consisted of a chain link cage with a padlock. When it got nearly full, we would transport the detainees to the real jail.

The Grand Marshall eventually came by our jail, assisted by a couple of drunks. He requested that we allow all the drunks in our custody to be set free. Needless to say, the number in our holding cage grew by three more. Capt. Woodlee didn't play that game.

Nowadays, the fair is a mere afterthought. Tampa University is back to normal and SEU is slinking around again fighting the ever present crime in the big city.

Captain Woodlee's Gas Caps

Capt. Woodlee was so loved by his police officers that they would do anything he asked, mostly without question.

Frank came to roll call one night and was lamenting. Some sorry bastard stole his gas cap. He forgot to mention the color of the cap.

When the shift was over there were gas caps for his car in every color available.

Duck Man

During a drug investigation conducted by the SEU we came in constant contact with a suspect who lived in Sulphur Springs. Every time we saw him he was surrounded by druggies, acting very much like a drug dealer. Thinking of the old saying, "If it looks like a duck and quacks like a duck, then it must be a duck", we nicknamed him "Duck Man" Every time we would see this jerk-weed come out in a bar we would "quack" at him.

He asked why.

We told him that every time we saw him he was with ducks. When we saw him drinking, he was with ducks. No matter where we saw him, ducks were around. We told him that we assumed that he must be a duck.

This mommy's boy had his mother complain to the Mayor's office. The office then contacted the Chief's office. The Chief told Capt. Woodlee and all members of SEU to stop quacking at this jerk wad.

Well, it didn't end there.

We soon formed a strange alliance with a bar owner who moved to Tampa from Tennessee. He opened a hip young person's bar which he named "The He & She Lounge". It was located near Christ the King Catholic Church. The lounge had a stand up Texas bar and a raised dance floor which lit up and kept time to the music the DJ was playing.

This lounge was a full liquor bar and the beer it only sold was cans of Schlitz Malt Liquor. No other beers were available.

The place was jammed on Friday & Saturday nights as the owner sponsored a mini-skirt contest on top of the bar. The winners were voted on by the applause of the patrons at the bar. The place was very popular with young men and police officers as well.

It didn't take long for the contestants to figure out that they had an advantage if they removed their panties before the contest began.

After we were directed to quit quacking at our suspected drug dealer, I came up with a brilliant idea.

One Saturday night while my druggie was in the lounge, I directed the DJ to stop in the middle of his next selection. He was to stop the song and to announce over the PA system, "For all you ducks out there, QUACK, QUACK!!"

This sent this nut over the edge!

The next night we hit his house with a warrant to search for drugs. Upon our arrival he was having a party. He made a loud announcement that we could search forever and find nothing since they had smoked it all up.

We bid them adieu, conveniently grabbed his vacuum cleaner, and then left. We went back to the station, laid out some newspaper, cut the vacuum cleaner bag open, and spread its contents out. We used tweezers to pick out suspected marijuana particles. After these particles tested positive for *cannabis sativa,* we traveled back to the party, and placed the elusive duck under arrest.

The next Friday night I traveled in my personal 1967 fire engine red Mercury Comet to park it on the lot of a popular south end night club. The place was called "Dante's Inferno."

I did this immediately after seeing our duck friend.

When I got there, I asked a young lady, "If I give you fifty dollars, would you purchase fifty dollars worth of marijuana from *The Duck?*"

She said that she would.

I then asked her to instruct him to put her purchased marijuana on the left front tire of her Red 1967 Comet in the parking lot.

She did just that. He followed her instructions precisely.

I arrested him and The Duck complained that I didn't have a search warrant to retrieve the marijuana.

When I explained to him that I really don't need a search warrant for my own car he wasn't very happy.

The Duck pled guilty finally and that ended the Duck Saga!!

III

The Brotherhood

These are several stories from my career.
I will attempt to keep the stories relevant.
Let's nickname this section,

*"Police Officers
Who Made A Difference
In My Life."*

Officer W. A. Williams

Officer W. A. Williams was a Spanish speaking redneck who would rather fight than eat. W. A. would just stand nearby to a problem listening.

He had an obvious "tell". The giveaway that W. A. was going to spring into action was when he would turn sideways, remove his front partial dental plate, and put it in his right front pocket. Then Shazam! Biff, bang, and the fur would fly.

One day I was involved off duty in an accident on my way home. I was driving a 1965 Volkswagen Bug. I was going south on MacDill.

As I approached Bay to Bay, a car with several children in the car pulled out in front of me. It was too sudden to avoid and I hit them fairly hard. Red liquid went all over the interior of their vehicle.

I thought it was blood.

During the impact, I had bent the steering wheel in half, and I broke the windshield as well when my left wrist struck it.

Amazingly enough, I only bruised my wrist.

My passenger door popped open and my service revolver skipped out of the car and into the middle of the intersection.

After I quickly retrieved my wayward gun, I began directing traffic and the driver of the car with the red liquid (which turned out to be Cherry Slurpee) started yelling at me, "Where did you come from?"

About that time W.A. showed up as the investigating officer. He gathered me up, put me in an ambulance, and had me transported to Tampa General where my angel nurse friends were waiting for me with open arms.

Richard Lee Cloud

These next few stories present very touchy subject matters. They are about Richard Lee Cloud. You'll have to decide whether he was a good cop, or a bad cop.

I will limit these stories to only a few, I rode with Dick Cloud so much that I probably could dedicate an entire book on just my experiences with him.

One day, while Dick and I were patrolling Port Tampa, he was asked to call home. After the call, Dick told me that, "We have to go to my house." He continued, "There's a rat running around in my living room and Wanda wants me to come home and kill it."

Well, when the "commander in chief" at home tells you to come home and kill a rat, you don't argue with her.

We were driving a 1964 dark colored Dodge at the time. It was not a fully decked out police vehicle. It was quite plain, in fact. All that we had was a portable blue light that sat on the dash board, if you positioned it just right.

Dick said, "Hold on to the light and your seat, Guinea!" With that said, we drove off to his house. It was in the four hundred block of Alva, which is near MLK and North Boulevard.

Once we arrived, we went inside where we found Wanda, a good looker, standing with both feet on the couch.

With our entry, the rat spotted us and ran up the drapes. Dick hit the rat with a nightstick which knocked it to the floor. With the rat on the floor, I jumped up and onto the couch with Wanda.

Dick finally dispatched the rat. This freed us up from rat extermination and we raced back to our area of patrol.

No one ever found out about what we did.

Dick and I were partnered up again. Just like last time, we found ourselves driving our patrol in a dark colored sedan.

That evening we were driving west bound on Hillsborough Avenue, near Habana Avenue. A marked Unit attempted to pull us over from about two blocks away.

Dick stated, "This is bull shit! He is not going to pull us over!" Off to the races we went. We never stopped and never identified ourselves.

The marked Unit radioed in that he was in a pursuit, going west on Hillsborough from Habana, and heading towards Town & Country. We never stopped and finally the pursuit vehicle gave up their chase.

Cloud decided that we were so far out of our zone that "We may as well take a ride to Clearwater Beach."

And that's exactly what we did!

We drove a Tampa police unmarked unit to the public parking area on Clearwater Beach and then back to Tampa.

That is, after we enjoyed the view for a while.

There was a young teenager that we were asked to arrest who resided on Rio Vista Street behind the Kash n' Karry grocery at the river. When we would approach this kid's house, he would run out of the house, down to and into the river, swim to the middle, float on his back, and shoot Dick his middle finger.

Oh! And he'd be laughing the entire time.

We were off for the weekend. When we got back on Monday, the little wise guy was still on the hot sheet.

Dick had a plan this time and told me, "You drive, Guinea! I have a surprise for that little shit this morning."

Dick took off his shoes and socks. He then rolled up his trousers, put his gun belt in the trunk, and directed me to pull up in front of the kid's house.

When the kid jumped into the river, things were different. Unknown to him, Cloud jumped in right behind him, when the little bugger thought he was going to shoot Dick the bird again, he got fooled, and he almost drowned.

This is the last saga that I will report involving R.L. Cloud.

There was a duplex in the eight hundred block of Braddock Street that was originally constructed several years before by two brothers for them to live in. The brothers owned the Tahitian Inn on Dale Mabry Highway.

This house had been occupied by a few infamous people. While several of these residents were living there, they became friends of mine and occasionally *informants* for lack of a better name.

While visiting this house one evening in a marked police unit, a strange event happened. After my visit I was driving away from the house on Braddock Street when I was stopped by an unmarked unit being driven by our Det. R. L. Cloud.

Dick inquired of me my reason for being there. After my answer, he advised me not to return to the house as it was under constant surveillance. He proceeded to tell me that they heard my conversation while I was there and they knew that I had been sitting on a bed.

Dick then informed me that there was a trunk under that very bed containing a million American dollars. The money was stashed there by two Argentina brothers named Davila. They were attempting to launder the money and they were fugitives from their native country where they were wanted for the killing of a police officer.

As hard headed as I was, and still am, I never returned physically to that house. I did keep in touch with both my informants by phone though, using the code name of "Flash."

Here's a fast forward update to this last story.

Thirty to thirty-five years had passed since then. While I was Supervisor in 911, Sergeant

Bill Todd walked up behind me, massaged my shoulders, and asked me, "How you doing 'Flash?'"

Corporal Robert Wheary

Corporal Robert Wheary assisted me on a call in Sulphur Springs. An older white male decided to shoot it out with a squad of police officers. This was not a wise idea.

The suspect shot through the door and struck our Sergeant three times in his upper left shoulder. I gathered up the Sergeant and dragged him behind a tree.

Corporal Wheary returned fire on this male and physically smashed thru the jalousies in the door. This forced the suspect to flee the residence by way of the back door. This is where he met his maker.

Corporal Wheary stopped a driver south bound over Jefferson Street. The driver resisted the initial stop and spit on the Corporal. He then ran down the interstate, climbed over the fence, and was running south on Jefferson Street.

Wheary left his zone car running and gave chase. We could hear Wheary yelling at the driver, "Pick it up, you SOB!"

Bob had thrown his night stick toward the suspect with the hope that the damn fool would pick it up. If he had, this would mean that he had armed himself. If he had picked it up, he would have met his Waterloo.

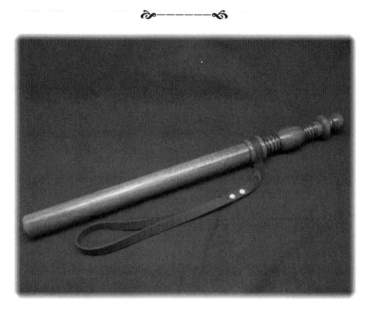

IV

Buddies
&
Partners

Here are some mentions and some quick stories about some colorful police officers I met and worked with over the years.

They're offered in no particular order.

Some of them were great. Some were almost great. Some, well, that you will have to make up your own mind about.

Ralph Whitley

Officer Ralph Whitley did things none of us would have thought were possible.

One night, while in his own vehicle, he announced over KIB459 that he was going to write the pilot of a private plane a ticket for attempting to land his plane at night at Peter O'Knight Airport.

In case you might not have gathered, Ralph was our department's internal entertainment.

He never let us down.

Jim Harris

Jim Harris was infamous for having the unique ability to get me in hot water almost every time I partnered up with him.

Let me cite just one of far too many possible gems as an example.

On one cold night, Jim tried to serve up a warrant to a not so cooperative recipient. While running after his target, he went through a yard and fell into a hole.

That hole was where a septic tank had been recently removed and not filled in properly.

Let's just say Harris made a big stink of it.

Jim Sigmon

Jim Sigmon was known to his close friends as "Siggypoo." He was a very pleasant and a naturally funny person. That being said, you would never know when you were going to become part of his humor.

He was absolutely loved by everyone.

Ronnie Slinker

Ronnie Slinker was an extremely large man. Add to this the fact that he had a 5th degree belt in Judo. He could and would hurt someone if they needed it.

Bobbie Flores

Bobbie Flores got noticed. His claim to fame was this: During Dick Greco's first term as Mayor, Bobbie went down to the public assistance office where he applied for and was granted *food stamps!*

Knowledge of this one act became so embarrassing to the "powers that be" that it shamed them into granting our department an actual decent wage.

For this I offer a belated and grateful "Thanks, Bobbie!"

Jerry Carter

Jerry Carter was a nice man and a pleasant squad member. If memory serves me correctly, he unfortunately was shot with his own gun. This occurred during a fight at his off duty job at the Tampa Theater.

Willie Monroe

Willie Monroe called me "Sal" ever since he had known me. Willie was the type of person you just had to like and even love. He was always smiling and always friendly.

If Willie ever had any occasion to shoot at you, you would not have any worries, especially if he was actually aiming at you. He could never hit you.

Rufus Lewis

Rufus Lewis was a friendly, well-educated Giant of a man. Unless unduly provoked, he was always even-tempered and considerate to all.

He was my friend to the end; even in our waning years.

Frank O. Gray

I called Frank Gray by the nickname "FOG." It should be extremely clear, by some of the stories that will soon follow, that I was incredibly fond of our friendship over the years.

There were so many great police officers whom I had the privilege to partner up with in various parts of town. One of these special places was Central Avenue

Until about 1967 or so, Central Avenue was a business area of town. It was a two block long street that was in the Black area of town near the train station.

The police officers there were always black officers. That was, until me.

I was privileged to serve on the first salt and pepper team ever to walk a beat together in this area.

I believe my first assignment was with Frank O. Gray, a black policeman with seniority over me. Over the years Frank and I became great friends and that friendship continues even now.

FOG, as I affectionately referred to him,

proved to be an incredibly caring & intelligent man; as well as a great police officer. Other parts of my Salt & Pepper teams were Elijah Dickson and Oscar Ayala.

Oscar was a native of Cuba who was a gentle giant of a man. He was feared, however, by the criminal element because when he told them to do or not do something they usually didn't understand him. When they didn't, the next thing they would feel was a bop on the head.

What made Central Avenue so unique was the characters and businesses that inhabited that neighborhood such as Lovey Beauty Shop, Moses White's Cozy Corner, The Cotton Club, Pop Joiners Place, The Greasy Spoon and, my favorite, The Little Savoy.

It was my favorite because my Father ran it for Mr. Italiano. This was done as a "personal favor" so that the owner, who had fallen ill, wouldn't lose his business.

The Central Avenue Beat

Here's another story that occurred on Central Avenue beat.

We had a call at the Cotton Club to assist the Tampa Fire Department. Upon our arrival we observed the Tampa Fire Department attending to a short stocky black male dressed in an off colored suit with a vest. The black male had been shot in his abdomen at close range with a twenty-five caliber hand gun. The bullet was stuck in this fellow's muscle. The firefighter was applying a butterfly bandage to the wound.

They were getting ready to transport the other part of the assault to Tampa General since he had the crap beat out of him.

How did this unfold?

The beat up guy shot the well-dressed guy for looking at his girlfriend in the Cotton Club. The idiot didn't know that he had shot Kid Gavalan – *the welter Weight Champion of the world from Cuba* – the champ couldn't speak English, but his fists didn't need to!

Here's just one more story about the Central Avenue team.

One day, Frank Gray and I were walking the beat together. That day we had been chasing a bunch of young "Jitterbugs" from the beat back into the projects. When we got off work, Frank asked me to join him for a beer. I accepted and told him I'd buy if we went over on Dale Mabry.

Frank wanted to go to the Cotton Club. I thought better of that idea as we had just spent eight hours "enforcing" the law on Central.

We both went our separate ways. The next night Frank told me that I should be glad I didn't go. When he pulled up and got out of his Volkswagen he was accosted by one of the kids that we chased earlier that day. The kid produced a straight razor and told FOG he was going to cut him. With that threat presented, FOG fired a gun that he had concealed in his coat pocket. The bullet went through the material of his jacket and the round found its way to the bad guy's crotch.

This folded the kid up like a two dollar suitcase and made him forget all about his razor blade.

V

Stories as Remembered

Captain E. D. Simmons

As new equipment would come to the forefront, especially if it was a new car, the brass on each shift wanted to try it out.

So, for instance, when the first "arrow car"[4] was placed in service, Captain Simmons broke it in. This made the brass very identifiable. When you saw the arrow car on the street, you knew who was driving it.

One night I was talking to an informant in the parking lot of the Seminole Library at Central Avenue and Osborne. My informant was driving her mom's new fire engine red Cadillac convertible and I was driving my assigned marked vehicle.

From the library parking lot, I saw Simmons' arrow car approaching. I didn't want him to have any knowledge of or contact with my informant. Currently he was in the dark about her. I truly didn't want my informant known.

So, I told her to take off and not stop until she arrived in Port Tampa. I wasn't stopping

---

[4] An "arrow car" had a lighted directional arrow sign that could be raised up about 10' in the air to direct traffic around an obstacle.

until I got to Lutz. I was very cautious with my sources.

We both took off like bats out of hell and with no headlights. Simmons got on the radio and demanded that the marked unit going north on Central Avenue, identify itself.

That was *not* going to happen.

Twenty years later, Captain Simmons and I were both retired and next to each other in a food line. I leaned over and whispered to him, "Marked unit going north on Central from Osborne, identify yourself."

He looked at me with a puzzled expression and asked, "Was that you, Guinea?"

DUI Counter Attack

One Friday afternoon I left home for roll call, which was to take place just before 7 pm. I have always been a believer in being early. If you're not fifteen minutes early, you are late. It's called "Sinatra Time."

When I got to the intersection of Armenia and MLK, I observed a white male stagger out of a bar, get in his car, and drive east on MLK. In police work, this was technically a "signal one," but it is also what we call "an easy score."

I advised my radio support that I would transport. Hell! That's where I was going anyway, right?

Driving east towards the bridge I observed another signal one. When I turned on the red lights I was right behind the vehicle. I watched as the driver and his passenger switched places. They did this *while driving.*

You guessed right if you believed they were both drunk.

Now, I've got three all in my back seat.

I advised my radio support that I'm 10-35 with three to booking.

Hell! I was going there, right?

As I turned south onto Tampa Street, I heard myself saying out load, "Damn! Another signal one!"

This time the guy driving turned left on a side street and was heading for Florida Avenue. He wouldn't pull over. I turned on the lights and activated the penetrator siren.

This time he stopped.

As this joker approached me, an awfully strong odor was emitting from him. He had defecated into his pants.

He received the long-distance roadside tests. He didn't pass.

After arresting *Mr. Poopoo Pants,* I placed him in my front seat to take him to jail.

At the risk of repeating myself, Hell! I was going there, Right?

Now I have four DUIs, with one packing a load. The station is less than a mile away from this point.

I can say without any reservations that it was the longest mile in my career.

When arriving at the breathalyzer room, there were several officers waiting their turn in line. When I announced that I was next up, they all told me that I wasn't anyone special and could wait my turn.

I put the four guys in the line and said, "Okay, I'll be outside waiting."

I decided to let the ramifications of their objections seep quickly into the room's ambiance.

Without much fanfare, the line-cutting objectors changed their minds and I was quickly promoted to *next in line!*

The results of my signal one activities needed to be addressed. It took three trustees two hours to clean my zone car of the rank odor.

Oh! I forgot to mention this one detail. All five of us threw up driving to the station that night.

DUI Story - Number Two

I was making a DUI arrest one time about 3 am at Gandy & Himes. At that time, I observed another really drunk driver on Gandy traveling towards me.

I couldn't stop him manually. As I finished up with the first DUI I was working on, this other drunk dummy drove past me going the other way.

I knew what I had to do as I thought to myself, "Now I got him."

I called for a backup and an Officer Luddy Dial responded to my request.

Officer Dial was an interesting guy. He had no neck and was about six feet tall. Luddy was also two hundred and eighty pounds big, a beer guy, and meaner than a snake.

I had tested the drunk driver and had him half way into the back seat. That was when Dial decides to slap his left leg and state, "You heard the officer! Get your God damn leg in the car."

I forgot to mention that the drunk was huge. What's more, this behemoth took offense at Dial's statement. He reached up and grabbed the roof of my squad car for leverage and exclaimed as he was coming out of the car: "You mother f___kers are going to have to kill me!"

With that out in the open, he came out all the way and the fight was on. He fought, bit, cursed, and spit at us. After one *hell of a fight,* he was finally subdued.

I can't recall a worse physical fight at any time of my career.

Lessons from Drunks

One of the perks of being on the DUI squad was that you could make extra money. We were hired to be present at all the mandatory schools associated with a DUI conviction.

During one session, a student, really just a chronic drunk, schooled me on a method he thought up that would enhance my number of arrests.

He told me the following:

"Obtain a wide magic marker, preferably black and a small tack hammer."

He encouraged me to add these two "tools" to my crime fighting weapons arsenal.

He told me to get a note pad for when I started my shift. He instructed me to go to the bar parking lots in my area and mark down the make, color and tag numbers of about five or six cars in my notebook and then leave for a couple of hours.

He continued, "Then make the rounds and return to those same bars and mark down the cars whose owners are still actively engaged in their bar activity. Then leave again. Go 10-10 (Get something to eat) if you have to."

He then said, "After eating, make the rounds to the same bar parking lots again, checking the list for who's been naughty and who's been nice."

The student added, "The crucial key to making this pay off is as follows: Mark any cars on any lot that were on the initial list either with a big "X" on the left front headlight or break the bulb out with your trusty tack hammer. Once done, leave again."

He continued, "Then, about two am, start driving the back roads near or around those bars. Look for cars with a left light with a big 'X' on it or no left front headlight at all!"

"When one is found, "Bingo!" you have a drunk!"

I can't tell you how many drunks I caught using this method, but at twenty-five arrests a week over a two-year stretch; I'll let you do the math.

The Peanut Butter Incident

Let's throw a note in here that will surely make the older guys and gals smile a little.

Does anyone of my friends remember the "Peanut Butter" incident involving a well-liked Sergeant?

Let me help jar your memory a bit. It involved placing peanut butter under the door handle of a police car. If that rings a bell for you, you will smile. If it doesn't, just pass on.

Richard Benitez

This next story will bring back memories and give those who weren't police officers an idea of some of the other pranks we played on one another.

During one evening shift, Richard Benitez came into Tampa General Hospital Emergency Room and asked me to help him perform a task. He was a Tampa ID technician.

Richard was a handsome man quite a bit overweight. He was so overweight that Martin's Uniforms couldn't supply one in his size. To solve the problem, the city allowed him to wear a Cuban Che Guevara shirt as a uniform shirt.

One night, Richard was tasked to fingerprint a cadaver in the morgue. He wasn't particularly comfortable being in one's presence, either.

Let me interject that when Richard got excited, he had a tendency to stutter.

As you old timers may or not recall, the entrance to the morgue was in the basement. It was through a door near the ER. The steps leading to the basement were a very narrow and steep set of concrete steps. They existed without

a hand rail. There was only one light switch located at the top of the stairs.

I hope this describes the atmosphere a bit.

I agreed to assist him and I accompanied our ID technician down the flight of stairs leading to the morgue. Once at the bottom of the stairs, Richard set up the equipment he needed to complete his assignment.

Unfortunately for him, he had his back to me and he couldn't see what I was doing.

While he was busy, I asked Richard the poor stiff's name and in which drawer number he might be located. Upon receipt of that 10-43 (information), I snuck up the stairs like a thief in the night and, on my way out, *I turned off the light.*

What a dirty rotten thing to do to a supposed friend!

You had to be there to hear Richard knocking over crap in his attempt to escape the ghosts of his imagination.

By the time Richard made it up the stairs, and back to the ER, he had sweated so much that his uniform shirt was soaked from the collar to the hem.

I've never heard so many swear words in my life. I must commend his command of language though. Richard cursed me in Spanish, in Cuban, and in English.

Fortunately, he was a forgiving person.

That being said, after that incident, our ID technician always sought help elsewhere.

Shots in the ER

During your career, did you have any occasion to administer an injection?

Yes, I mean giving a shot using a syringe.

Let's go back to the ER.

The ER used to have curtained off cubicles instead of rooms. As an officer, you might be fortunate or unfortunate to be assigned to the ER. This was to assist on the usually busy Friday or Saturday evening or midnight shifts. The ER could be as hectic as a regular zone during these times.

One Saturday night, a teenager was brought into the ER. I distinctly remember he was wearing Levi jeans. This kid was higher than a kite.

The ER doctor was attempting to give him a sedative to bring him back to earth.

To my surprise the young Doctor lost his patience. He was fed up with this kid's nonsense.

The doctor didn't flinch and handed me the charged syringe. He instructed me to stick the needle thru this kid's jeans and into either cheek of his ass and push the plunger.

I accommodated the young doctor gladly as I had become quite fond of this jerk as well.

Night Time Visitor

Do you remember when I stated that different types of police services were rendered according to where you lived?

Good! Here is an example of just that.

It was two in the morning when we received a call. There was a body lying on the grass between a ribbon driveway on Morrison Avenue. It was a pretty nice area of town and we seldom received calls in this neighborhood.

I was with a younger officer who clamored to me, "I want to drive! Can I?"

Being an old salt by now, and hating to drive, I made out as if I were giving him a treat. He fell for it and took to the wheel like a kid to candy.

When we arrived at the address, the rookie started to pull into the driveway. It was only at that moment when I remembered the call stating there was a person *lying on the driveway.*

The very one we were about to drive into!

Luckily we didn't run the person over.

We got out of our car and approached the body. Upon closer examination, we found out that it was a young white male. He was unresponsive, with four to five gunshots in his back.

But he was still alive!

We called an ambulance immediately and then our Supervisor. It was not Woodlee this time.

I walked to the rear of the residence and encountered what appeared to be a thirty year old white male. He was at the top of a set of metal stairs leading up to a garage apartment located above the garage. This guy was clothed in a bathrobe with bedroom slippers. He was standing on a landing high above me.

This gentleman was speaking very calmly while holding a twenty-two caliber semi-automatic in his right hand.

I inquired of him, "Do you know anything about the body out front?"

He retorted with great surprise, "Do you mean I hit him?"

I said, "Yes. It appears that you did."

I then asked him if he would please remain where he was while I tended to the guy on the driveway.

After attending to the victim and shipping him off to the ER at Tampa General Hospital, I returned to interview the man with the gun.

His story line went like this: The previous night, he had been in bed with his wife. His wife awakened him just in time to see someone on the landing attempting to open their door. The suspect had his hands through the glass on the door & was unlocking the door from the inside. Mr. homeowner armed himself, turned on the porch light, and opened the door.

The suspect turned and attempted to flee down the narrow stairwell.

The now armed homeowner used the railing of the stairs to steady the gun and fired seven rounds of 22 caliber LR at the idiot, striking the suspect four to five times. No charges were filed. This was a great example of the "Castle Doctrine."

The homeowner also owned and operated the Pro Shop at a local Bowling Alley. His surname, as I recall, was *Sardengna*.

Believe it or not, this saga continued on.

My favorite Supervisor, Frank B. Woodlee, got involved.

This time he just happened to be in the ER on probably Monkey business.

I told him that I needed some help. He, being my friend, was always ready to help, aid, and assist his favorite "Guinea."

The damn fool with the gunshot wounds that we found in the driveway survived his wounds.

Unfortunately, he almost died from the treatment, or maybe mistreatment, in the ER.

What happened?

This damn fool spat saliva mixed with blood all over Frank's uniform shirt. He was being set upright so that the necessary x-rays prior to surgery could be obtained.

That's when he spat at Woodlee.

That was when Frank directed me to obtain a roll of adhesive tape and bring it back to him.

Well, you guessed it. We taped that jerk while he was sitting up. We made sure that he could not spit at anyone else.

We taped everything shut - everything except his nostrils.

A Snake in the Barrel

One of the specialty units that I was invited to be a part of again was commanded by Captain Frank B. Woodlee. The Sergeant was H.B. Maxey and the Corporal was John Bright.

This unit was manned by eleven hand-picked Tampa Police Officers, twelve HCS Officers and twelve Florida Highway Patrolman. We all worked DUI's under the direct control & direction of the University of South Florida. The program was financed by a federal grant under the auspices of Dr. Blount.

All vehicles, equipment, and training were paid for through the grant. This included reimbursing the city for our salaries. We were the first Tampa Police officers to have take-home cars. This made others envious of our good fortune.

We only handled DUIs. Since there were only thirty-three officers between the three agencies, we each had to operate the breathalyzer room at least once during the duration of the operation. We called the room, "The Barrel."

On my night in the barrel, I was attempting to administer a test on an inebriated subject. The testing was conducted in a small six foot by six foot room with only one door in or out.

My Sergeant, H B Maxey, stood in the door way and advised me that the shift commander wanted him to bring my gun to him.

As would any self-respecting police officer, I told Maxey I wasn't giving him or anyone my service revolver.

The Sergeant persisted and persisted, aggravating me enough that I emptied my gun, put the bullets in my pocket, and reluctantly surrendered my gun to Maxey.

No sooner did the Sergeant step out of the doorway than another policeman appeared in the doorway *with a ten-foot, live boa constrictor around his neck.*

I jumped up on my chair at the same time that the drunk subject did. Apparently, we were both deadly afraid of snakes.

I informed the cop with the snake that he couldn't beat my ass and that he had better get out of the door jam. He did just that and I took the rest of the shift off.

Yes. I admit it. It was a sneaky way to get out of running breathalyzers.

ॐ-------ॐ

Fort Homer Hesterly Armory

Police officers salaries never were very large, but the perks and the adrenaline produced by

the job offset the money shortage. Many of us took on off-duty jobs as a way to offset our poor pay. I was no exception to this. I worked almost every off-duty job offered for extra money.

The job that I was offered by the Fort Homer Hesterly Armory occurred every Tuesday night. That was when the wrestling matches took place.

I got to see a freak show in person every Tuesday night. A freak show being performed for people who really believed that crap was real.

Entertaining? Yes! Real? Are you serious?

I have met The American Dream (Dusty Rhodes), The Great Malenko, Andre the Giant, Dirty Dick Murdock, Wahoo McDaniels, the Bristol Brothers, Gorgeous George, and Eddy Graham.

While working the matches one evening, I was approached by a Hillsborough County Civil Deputy Sheriff. He had a writ of replevin for Dusty Rhodes' Cadillac which was painted like the American Flag. This sheriff assured me that if Dusty interfered he would surely arrest him. He proceeded to do what he came to do – repossess the vehicle.

Dusty found out and came running out to protest the impounding of his car. He soon decided the sheriff wasn't kidding and returned to the ring. The officer was clearly relieved by this. He didn't want to put Dusty in jail or have to try to deal with an arrest.

As an aside, in about 1990, I began working full time for Lazydays RV Supercenter. A young man who drove a tractor for Lazydays approached me and asked me if I ever worked the wrestling matches as a Tampa Police officer. He informed me that when he was about ten years old he would find me at the matches on Tuesday night and he would ask me to let him into the matches because he didn't have the funds to purchase a ticket. This young man told me I never refused his request and for that consideration he offered me his help if I ever needed it. This was a nice consideration for just being nice.

I once approached Andrc the Giant while I was working plain clothes in SEU. I did not know at that time that he was French and that he spoke no English. I mistakenly placed my hand on his back to say, "Hello." Was I ever taken by surprise! As soon as I touched his back, Andre reached around, grabbed me by my shirt, and picked me bodily up off the ground.

I quickly told the owner of the lesbian bar to tell him I was a plain-clothes cop and that he was in serious jeopardy of getting shot!

She convinced him and he put me down.
He did.
This was a smart move on his part.

Dog Track Memory

I once knew a young black male who, as a teenager, was a nice young man. Unfortunately, as often happens, he went astray and he ultimately made enough bad choices that he ended up in prison.

Time marched on.

One night, while I was working the dog track, this young man approached me and asked me if I remembered him from years past.

I told him that I did recall knowing him from several years prior.

As he approached me this time, he was dressed in a white suit, white shoes and hat, and was wearing a gold grill on his teeth.

We exchange superficial pleasantries and soon parted.

Later on that night, he found me again and asked me if he could "hold twenty."

The term, "hold twenty", was street jargon for "will you give me twenty dollars?"

I reluctantly surrendered my hard-earned twenty to him, no questions asked.

He looked at my badge number and stated that he was going to buy a Trifecta ticket with the twenty I gave him and he was going to play "4-6-8."

That was my badge number.

The race ran and the billboard lit up. It stating that there was only one winner on the Trifecta.

The winning numbers were "4-6-8" and it paid out $2200.

Soon afterward, here came my pimp. He was looking *very friendly,* with a fist full of money.

He chased me across the first floor of the track, all the time attempting to give me ten percent.

Finally, I quit running and gathered up the two hundred and twenty dollars with as little fan fare as possible.

Christmas Party

The chief of Police's secretary, Peggy, asked me if I would be Santa Claus for the Christmas party. It was going to be given for all the ladies that worked at 1710 Tampa Street. The party was going to be held at Busch Gardens in the Swiss House. It was going to be a swank venue.

After Peggy assured me that they would rent a professional Santa suit, I agreed to be Santa. I did this because it would not have been a good career move on my part to turn it down.

I had a friend at this time of my life that was a civilian drinking buddy. His street name was "Wee." I asked him to accompany me on this errand and Wee agreed. Off to the party we went.

I swore Wee in as my partner and gave him my badge, handcuffs, and gun as the Santa Outfit didn't have any pockets.

The party itself was stressful because of my own foolishness.

I admit it. I got very drunk. I know that's hard to believe.

I compounded the problem even further.

Once we left the party, I asked Wee to take me to any and all bars in our path.

Well, we visited many bars on the way home. They included straight bars, gay bars, and yes, even lesbian bars.

We went by the police department, Santa suit and all, where Sergeant Riley Maseada noticed me *three sheets to the wind* in the lobby.

He had me handcuffed and took me to booking. That's where they played along with the joke, printed me, and took my mug shot.

The Super Bowl was scheduled and there

were prostitutes from Atlanta in town. Two of the whores from Atlanta were arguing with a matron about their bond when they discovered my drunk ass sitting on a bench.

One whore told the other, "Shit man! They even arrested Santa, shut up girl."

At that, I stood up, gained my balance, and announced, "Ho! Ho! Ho! You don't know! Santa gotta go! Open the door!"

The guard heard me, came up, opened the door, and I left.

On the way home we stopped at the last bar. It was the Red Clemente's Lounge.

Upon entering, we were greeted by a very familiar person and frequent patron. It was none other than a popular attorney in Tampa, "Elvin Martinez."

Noticing the Santa gctup, he asked me if I would go to his house and greet his two infant children. He wanted me to reassure them of

Santa Claus's existence.

It didn't matter to him that Santa was "Shit faced" drunk.

I accommodated my friend's request.

VI

Tampa Natives

Here are a few delightful people whom I encountered when the job threw us into close contact.

Almost Native

I'm almost a Tampa native. My parents brought me to Tampa from Quincy, MA. This occurred when I was only one year old. We had followed the rest of my father's relatives in the food industry here at that time.

When coming to Tampa in the early 1940s, my family operated open air fruit markets, Italian restaurants, bars, and a pool hall near the University of Tampa. Even a fancy Italian Restaurant on Indian Rocks Beach was ours to operate at one time.

I'm proud to say that that's where I learned whatever meager cooking skills that I possess today.

My father, Amato "Al" Severino, was one hell of a man. He never allowed me to know that the family wasn't super wealthy by going without. I always had anything and everything I needed or wanted.

My mother, Marcella, was from Boston. She was the daughter of Lithuanian immigrants. She was the type of humble God fearing person that would suddenly develop a dislike for pumpkin pie if there was only one piece left.

I hope that you have been blessed with at least one such person in your life.

During my formative years, I was raised around adults; all friends of my parents. At a very young age I was exposed to scenarios that were usually reserved for an adult population. I was allowed to be a child but under the direction and personal supervision of "Al" Severino.

I truly believe in my heart of hearts that my father molded me into the man I am today; good, bad, or indifferent.

For those of you who have shared my police officer existence, you know what I'm talking about.

Let's jump ahead and talk about how this relates to this story line.

Do you remember the little piece that I mentioned earlier about my father being Mr. Salvatore "Red" Italiano's friend and companion?

Well, the relationship was a little bit more than what I had first let on.

My father loved that man beyond belief. On far too many Sundays and holidays to count, our family would visit the Italiano family at their home on Fremont Street near Cass. This is where we would enjoy the best Sicilian food in Tampa, prepared by Nana, "Red," and his daughter.

The relationship was close and enjoyable.

Well, as we all must experience life changes, Mr. Italiano moved away. He eventually passed on while living out of the country. Mr. Italiano's remains were brought back home and interred at a cemetery on Buffalo Avenue and 50th Street.

On the Monday after his services, I, a fully grown man and a member of the Tampa Police Department, was summoned to Chief Charles Oteros's Office. Upon arrival, I was astonished to be confronted by Chief Otero and Sergeant Jack DeLlana. He was the Chief's cousin and our department's secret photographer.

While I was there in the office, I was shown about ten 8x10 inch black & white glossy close-up photos of attendees at Mr. Italiano s funeral service. You guessed it! I was in a bunch of the pictures.

When I was asked a leading question, I responded with a very respectful answer.

I was quickly dismissed from that meeting, and rightly so. We will leave it at that. You can come to your own conclusions.

A second visit to Chief Otero's office occurred again on a Monday morning. This time it was without the secret photographer.

It was about a complaint he received from the woman.

Her story follows.

114

Speaking Habla

One thing I regret not doing while living in Cigar City is learning to speak Habla better. I knew just enough Spanish, besides the typically used bad words, to get myself in serious trouble.

One mid-morning, I responded to a house owned by an older lady. She was complaining about several black youths. While walking past her house, they stole avocados from her tree.

Her tree's branches were hanging over the sidewalk which made them ripe for easy taking.

I had made every attempt to reason with this non-English speaking person and I didn't have any luck.

Finally, in a frustrating effort to end this conversation, I said to her, "Ma'am, if these kids spit in your face, and I didn't see them do it, I couldn't arrest them either for that".

Well, that Turkey didn't fly. She related to Charlie that I said I was going to spit in her face.

A note to all future residents: *If you want to live in Tampa, please become bilingual at least.*

Officer George Mishauf

This story is out of order but should be shared.

Officer George Mishauf, a northern transplant, and I were going to have lunch. This was known as 10-10 when provided as a code to radio dispatch.

We decided that we would eat at a famous establishment on 22nd Street Causeway.

The lunch location was known as "The Sea Breeze." It was owned and operated by an Italian by the name of George Licata.

Officer Mishauf and I asked to be seated next to a front window to give us a view of our marked zone car.

Being an almost native of Tampa I was intimately familiar with the menu, which was extensive. I ordered a simple pressed Cuban and a deviled crab and a Coke to wash it down.

When George placed his order, he pointed to the soft shelled crab item and gave me a look as if to say, "Should I order this?"

I shook my head indicating it was "not a good choice."

George looked at me with a "why not?" expression.

My response was this. "Although I'm told it's very flavorful and popular, the damn thing looks like a large spider on a bun."

I added, "Don't do it, George!"

Well, George would have none of my discouragement and didn't follow my advice. He ordered this tarantula sandwich and, upon its arrival, vacated the building and threw up next to our zone car in the parking lot.

It's a true story; I swear!

Internal Affairs

I want to make sure that I addressed an important issue, while I have my mind on it.

Although we had a weak internal affairs bureau, we had many clandestine or hatchet men who worked behind the scenes. They were as influential as any review board.

Every department has their share of colorful individuals. Each of them has had pasts of their own, all unique to themselves.

I have some knowledge of them, although not volumes. They're just tidbits of some of the shenanigans that took place when these big shots were coming up through the ranks.

Being of Sicilian descent and being raised by "Al" Severino, these various tidbits will go with me to the grave.

There is absolutely no merit or reason to besmirch the character or reputation of anyone just because you can.

Charlie "Brown"

Charlie "Brown" was a department head. He became known by this name in the media for one reason or another. Charlie was a fair person who led our Department with grace.

The Sea Breeze

While we are on the subject of the Sea Breeze, let's continue on.

I've made reference early on in this writing as to how we police officers all supplement our poor salaries by working off-duty jobs whenever offered. Well, Mr. Licata offered us opportunities on a regular basis.

He hired Tampa Police Officers to police his drive-in during the weekends. He didn't know it at the time, but most of us would have worked it for no pay.

You see, George Licata had a twenty-eight year old red-headed daughter named "Nica".

She was drop-dead gorgeous. She is my friend to this day and I am not lying when I say that she is as pretty now as she was back in the day.

But I digress.

These side jobs usually paid three dollars and fifty cents per hour. They were more perilous then our usual police jobs. What made them more perilous was the fact that we had to use our personal cars and we didn't have any way to call for help, if we needed it, other that a landline.

Now that I have set the stage, let me tell you what happened.

It was on a Saturday night. I was walking the

parking lot at the Sea Breeze and I was minding everyone's business. It was at that time that I observed a bunch of rowdy Palmetto Beach wannabe crooks around a vehicle being driven by a tender-aged girl who was obviously drunk.

When this group was told by me to shut the car off and to stop their foolishness, I was told to go make love to myself and in such a way that one might take offense.

There were about twenty jerks total.

They asked me what I was going to do about their behavior. They also pointed out that I was flying solo and that I was outnumbered twenty to one.

It was about that time that Mr. Licata saw that his hired security professional was about to get into some deep guacamole.

Realizing my predicament, he exited the kitchen area and came out onto the parking lot pavement.

He was not alone! He was accompanied by an old rabbit-eared 12 gauge double-barreled shotgun, make & model unknown.

It's wonderful sights like these that you can always tell when an employer truly cares for his hires.

Mr. Licata politely informed this Motley crew that anyone who accosted yours truly would be blown into the adjacent Palm River.

With the crew being guarded, I called for backup

When the Cavalry arrived, I arrested the whole damn group.

Thank you, Mr. George! And thank you, Nica, for the pleasant memories.

Tony Licata

While on the Licata family, let me mention this: George's brother, Tony, was also in the food business, as well as various real estate ventures.

Mr. Tony Licata owned and operated a Steak house named the Flaming Sword. It was located in the basement of a building on Tampa Street. The Flaming Sword was one of my favorite steak houses.

The Licata family was a well-loved part of our town and its Italian heritage.

Gladys

Gladys was a local civilian; a black female who truly loved us white law enforcers. She would lovingly refer to us as her "pink meat" police officers.

121

I personally nicknamed Gladys "Happy Butt" (Get it? "Happy Butt... Glad Ass.)

Gladys lived close to Tampa Street and Columbus Drive. She had a ritual way of meeting new police officers. There was a bunch of us, including myself, who were introduced to her – *all in the same manner.*

For the introduction to work, your training officer had to be privy to and part of this initiation. Without his help and fervent cooperation, it never would have occurred.

Your training officer had to make sure that you, the rookie, were riding passenger. He had to make sure that Gladys was up for and in on the joke too. She also had to be in the parking lot of the Blue Ribbon Super Market located at Columbus Drive and Tampa Street.

They pulled this initiation off as if they had a script to follow.

It always worked out well.

It would start when the trainer would summon Gladys over to the passenger window. When she came up to the window, he would say, "Gladys, I want to introduce you to Joe Severino. He's a new police officer."

When the trainee would turn to greet her, she would do one of two things. She would either stick a bare breast in the trainee's face or reach in and grab him by his crotch.

Either way, the trainee was faced with an immediate question: *What do I do now?*

That was the introduction to Gladys that many of us got.

Gladys was a good friend to us. She was a massive source of information into the criminal element of the city.

She knew the area and its history.

I'm glad she was our friend.

It was rumored that Gladys did hard time for shooting another person over change not rendered.

Here's another story from the same neighborhood. It has a different gender this time and, I swear, there's no crotch grabbing either!

Chester Lightburn

Chester Lightburn was a black male who had done time for armed robbery. He was really close to many of our police officers, including myself.

Chester would sometimes call one of us on the phone to report criminal activity in the area. He would tell us that there would be a bunch of men shooting dice in a particular bar, which he would then identify.

He would then say to us, "But first, give me thirty minutes before you show up."

Chester had a routine. He would go to the bar he had just reported. He would start the very crap game that he just reported. He would then fade out of the game and leave the area as fast as he could.

There were many gambling cases that came through our department that originated in this fashion.

There was an unwritten rule between gamblers and cops. If you ran and we caught you, you didn't fight us. Alternatively, if we chased you and you got away, we wouldn't pursue you any further. With rare exception, the rules of the game played out with everyone respecting the rules.

Chester was married to a heavy-set lady named "Essie Mae." They ran a small restaurant on Columbus Drive near Highland.

One morning, Essie Mae told Chester that one of her customers had stolen her purse. Chester obtained the names of the three customers from Essie and, by his own personal process, decided who the purse thief most likely was.

You seldom hear of this weapon anymore, but Chester owned one. Contemplate this... a convicted felon in possession of a ten gauge shotgun. I threw this tidbit of information in here so that you can make the connection necessary to fill out what occurred next.

Chester found his suspect. When he did, he hit him upside his head with the barrel of an unidentified weapon. He made him retrieve Essie's purse from where he threw it. He then shoved the black male down the middle of Highland Avenue, and directly to the police department. This is where he  turned the bad guy over to the first cop he found.

We never did try to find out how Chester *persuaded* this thief to remain steadfast and patient in his trip to the first police officer they encountered.

Palmetto Beach

Palmetto Beach was the area of town located south of Adamo Drive. It was a narrow portion of land which housed everything possible. You'd find there residential, industrial, warehouses, and retail stores. Included in the mix were bars, sandwich shops, and assorted restaurants.

The area even had it own drive-in movie named "The Auto Park." It was an often-shared rumor at the time that good girls didn't go on dates to the Auto Park.

I had the pleasure of meeting a great hard-working family of Sicilian immigrants who lived in that area. They were probably second generation. This great family consisted of a husband, a wife, and a teenage son "Tommy."

They all lived in a clean but modest home. Mom worked in a school cafeteria and Dad was a school janitor. Both parents spoke broken English.

From their actions it was very apparent that their son was their reason for living and the apple of their eye.

Once I really got to know their son, it became obvious to me that he was basically a really good kid.

Tommy was very knowledgeable about the mechanics of automobiles. This was attested to by the one he drove.

He actually built his ride, which as I recall was a beefed-up Chevy. By the time Tommy got done working on it, it was a muscle car that could haul ass.

Unfortunately, his work made it unusually loud.

You could hear Tommy coming into the neighborhood by the sound of his hot rod. Other officers, not knowing Tommy as I knew him, attempted to do their jobs by enforcing the traffic laws of the state of Florida.

They were extremely frustrated by Tommy. He would race throughout Palmetto Beach. He did this a lot! When they were able to catch and stop Tommy, they would attempt to either issue him a speeding ticket or, worse, arrest him.

At the time, I was a senior officer in the area. I was also well-liked by my peers. When I showed up during their traffic stops, they would cut Tommy some slack and just warn him.

After I retired, I found out that Tommy Cagnina had continued to work in the auto industry. He opened up and maintained a serious car engine business that reworked engines, heads, valves, and related motor repairs.

Tommy's business has been and still is located on 22nd Street near 3rd or 4th Avenue.

Years later, I attended a party at a friend of mine's house. During the event, I was introduced to a tall, dark-haired young man with a great personality.

From the moment I met him, this young man reminded me of a young man I knew years ago named "Tommy Cagnina."

Surprisingly enough, I found out that this new acquaintance turn out to be none other than Tommy 's son.

Rick Casares

In one way or another and because of their stature, Tampa Florida over the years was and is known to be the home of some larger than life characters. One such person who was associated with our community was a giant of a man named "Rick Casares."

While attending high school in Tampa, Rick was like a grown man playing with children. He set records in every sport he participated in.

Rick graduated from high school and went on to the University of Florida in Gainesville where he continued his sporting prowess.

Rick was eventually drafted by the Chicago Bears where he had a stellar career.

I became personal friends with this myth of a man and I was part of his life while he lived in Tampa after he retired from professional football. While Rick was a Florida Gator, some locals invited Rick to go with them Tarpon fishing. He drove down to Tampa bringing a non-descript gym bag with him. The locals took him in a boat to catch a tarpon, and catch one they did.

As this angler was reeling in this one hundred pound plus fish, Rick got excited, he pulled out of his gym bag a 35 caliber snub nose revolver, and shot the fish.

Rick became good friends with Cousins Guido and Louie Caggiano. I got to tag along with a group they hung out with because of their association, which included Rick and his lovely wife.

While being married, Rick was asked by his wife what he wanted for one of his birthdays.

His response was, "I'd like a top notch night club and I'll name it the 'Huddle.'"

Rick soon became the owner of the *Huddle Lounge* on North Dale Mabry Highway which became a showpiece for the city's entertainment center. Rick was the consummate gentleman always. Rick was a very soft spoken person who was always cordial and accommodating to everyone with whom he came in contact.

Suzie

During an SEU investigation we were introduced to a phone booth burglar. The thief really surprised us all, once we apprehended him, or her or it!!

Let me explain.

Officer Alvarez had secured a search warrant for a nicely appointed house located in Port Tampa. The house was a rental unit with the owner living in the house next door.

We decided that this operation would be best executed early in the morning while it was dark. Also, we needed several extra police to make the event go smoothly.

It was a cold night. There was dense penetrating moisture in the air.

The house had a front door that was half glass. As we approached the house, our own judo expert went to the front and announced our presence and that we had a search warrant.

Ronnie Slinker thought he saw a man standing in the doorway. He picked up a roll of roofing paper and threw it, breaking the door and knocking a heavy bust of Julius Caesar to smithereens.

Officer Jim Harris and I ran for the rear of the house. As we did, an overweight big blonde guy came running out the back door.

This moose had a full beard and he was barefooted and bare-chested wearing nothing but camouflage pants.

I was about to tackle this behemoth when a small female ran out of the house into the back yard yelling "Run Suzy run."

I was taken aback.

As I was recovering from this distraction, Suzy, or whatever it was, climbed over a chain link fence into an adjoining orange grove, escaping my grasp.

When Sergeant John Francis Branegan was giving me hell for not pursuing Suzy into the abyss, I assured him that I would find the person of interest before we left the area.

A search warrant soon produced our desired result. Coffee cans of change, nickels, dimes, & quarters were all over the place.

(I'll quickly add a tie-in here. In addition to this successful find, the warrant also produced the powder keg that almost blew up on me in the next story. There will be more on this to follow soon enough.)

After finding the booty, we found another type of booty. One bedroom was equipped as a torture chamber. It contained chains, whips, handcuffs, and yes, surprisingly enough, several dildos.

One of them was secured, separately from the others, for a specific purpose.

I went next door to the landlord's house and he gave up Suzy's identification in a Minnesota minute.

Suzy was soon facing the wall on a single size bunk bed taking up the entire mattress. From what I could see, our usual handcuffs were not going to fit this person's tree truck sized wrists. So, I walked up to this blob in the basket, put the cold barrel of a twelve gauge in his available ear, racked the shotgun, and then assured Suzy that should he decide to resist I would surely take his life.

Suzy became very cooperative from that moment on.

This search warrant occurred close to Christmas. As was stated previously, Captain Frank B. Woodlee was more than my supervisor. He was my much-valued mentor, my trusted friend, and, at times, my Guardian Angel.

What happened next was my idea and I take full responsibility for the outcome.

I wrapped that separated-from-the-herd "dildo" in a Christmas present fashion. *I even included a bow!*

It was at roll call on the night that I was going to present this gift to him that things changed rapidly. I think he smelled a rat or someone ratted me out.

Either way it was fortunate that things unfolded as they did.

Woodlee's first words from the podium at roll call were, "The dumb SOB who gives me that missing Dildo in any shape or form will be fired on the spot. Any questions?"

I believed what he said as gospel because when Frank Woodlee told you he was going to do anything, you could make bank on his word. So I raised my hand and waited for it.

When finally asked, "Yeah Severino. What is your question?"

I then raised the wrapped present up into the air for all to see and then asked permission to throw it in the garbage can.

Woodlee told me, "Severino, that's the smartest thing you've done lately."

Mr. Walters

As I had stated before, the city of Tampa had its share of very giving people among our citizenry. One of those genuinely giving businessman, was a fellow named, "Mr. Jim Walters."

My father and I had a conversation about Mr. Walters one time and my father told me that everything he knew about him was terrific. He said that Jim was a very endearing person.

I can vouch for that. Here's a story that I was personally involved in.

While living where I live to this day, I had a family who lived right next door. This family consisted of a father, mother, and two teenage kids; a 12 year old son named "Steven" and a younger daughter named "Kendra."

This family was very tight knit. They were a religious-oriented Sunday church and Sunday school attending type family.

We found out that Steven became ill. He was eventually diagnosed with terminal leukemia. The doctors in Tampa arrange for Steven to receive treatment at Saint Jude's hospital. It was being run by Danny Thomas as a research hospital solely for terminal children.

During the time that Steven was ill, he became very interested in airplanes and anything that had wings.

At that time, the Tampa police department had its own fixed wing named "Tillie" and several bell helicopters in our fleet. There was no problem getting Steven several trips in all of the TPD's Air Force.

Trying to give Steven a better flying experience, I asked myself, "Who do I know who has a jet plane?"

Mr. Jim Walters' name came to my mind. So, I called his main office and was intercepted by his executive secretary. After hearing Steven's story, she explained to me that Mr. Walters would surely not grant my request. That being said, she would advise him of my request for Steven and that she would get back with me on the following Monday.

I had no choice but to accept that answer.

Upon returning to work on Monday, I had a message to call the lady at Walters Incorporated.

When I called, I was told that Mr. Walters wanted to talk with me personally.

When we finally connected, Mr. Walters asked me, "Is this Corporal Severino?"

I responded, "Yes, it is. Is this is Mr. Walters, the millionaire?"

He stammered and replied, "Yes. This is Jim Walters."

As my father had advised me, Mr. Walters took Steven and seven of his family members and friends to Boca Raton and back. He also gave Steven a very nice gift as well.

Steven thanked me for making all the arrangements and said, "Joe, Mr. Walters sure drinks a lot of tomato juice."

I'll leave it up to you to figure what he was really saying.

&<----->&

Taking Care of the Dog

This story just came to mind. There was a gentleman named, "Primo," who was raised and lived in Ybor City. He owned and operated several liquor bars in Tampa Bay area and his brothers were also involved in the entertainment industry as well.

The elder of the brothers had been invited to attend President Fulgencio Batista's daughter's wedding. It was being held in Havana Cuba on the weekend.

While he was going to be absent from Tampa for several days, he asked one of his closest associates to "Take care of my dog while I'm gone."

As you might have gathered, those exact words have entirely different meaning depending upon who you are.

When the owner of the large black and brown Doberman pinscher inquired as to the whereabouts of his prized possession, he receiving this answer:

"Boss, you told me to take care of it!"

VII

Six Mile Creek Characters

These were not people who you wanted to hang around with.

The Safe Man

Eugene O.C. Austin was a safe man. He was a typical six mile creeker as well.

He visited Tampa from the Sarasota area occasionally. Eugene was a big guy who had a wandering eye from some type of eye disease.

One night, Mr. Austin strapped a horse saddle on the roof of his car, got into the saddle, and had another idiot drive him down 7th Avenue.

Needless to say, we stopped him very shortly after we became aware of his escapades.

We likely saved his life.

But it was a sight to behold while he was in the saddle.

The Car Thief

There was a young man who, for the purposes of this story, we'll call "Norman." He was a typical six mile creeker.

Norman was not your model citizen. He was far from it. Norman was a burglar and car thief. His chosen profession was a bit of a challenge for him because he was a little slow when it came to life skills.

This challenge made it easier for us.

After working all night in the Creek and harassing Norman the entire shift, Jim Sigmon and I decided to return to The Creek in Jim's personal car.

Observing Norman hitchhiking on Seventh Avenue, we stopped and picked him up.

Unfortunately for Norman, he didn't recognize us as the cops he had encountered earlier. He felt so comfortable with us that he asked where we stole the car we were driving.

He then asked where we were going to drop it off so that he could go get it – *poor soul.*

Catch Me If You Can

Jabo Giddens worked at a tire shop on 7th Avenue. In his youth, he was quite a character. Jabo had a new Mustang.

One weekend he drove this hot rod to Harold's Drive-In. He approached Officer R. L. Cloud and I and made a bet with us.

Jabo boasted that we had to give him a five car head start. After he was five car lengths out, we could try to catch him.

What was the wager?

If we caught him, he would give us no hassle. He would plead guilty and we could put him in jail.

However, if he outran us, we wouldn't take out a warrant or make any reprisals – none whatsoever.

Well, he got away. He drove east out into the county, got out of his Mustang, and gave Cloud his middle finger.

This continued.

The next weekend the same game was offered. However, this time when Jabo crossed into the county there were three Hillsborough County Sheriffs waiting for him.

As you might have surmised, a bet is a bet and off to jail he went.

❧––––––❦

The Web

While walking beat numbers six & seven in Ybor City, you learned several tricks to make it less stressful. If you did these tricks well, then walking the beat became fun and games!

There was a very scary alley on the south side of 7th Avenue. It was "L" shaped with buildings on both sides of the "L." A police officer confided to us that he would bring a spool of thread from his wife's sewing machine with him sometimes. When he would check the building at the beginning of his tour of duty, he would put thread from the bricks on one building to the other side forming a spider web like effect.

He would do this on both openings. When he arrived back, he would check his webs with a flashlight to see if they were broken.

He should not have told us about that part. After we found this out, we would drive by the alley and use a night stick to knock his spider web down. We would then wait for the call which always started out with, "Send me a backup. Someone's in my alley!

Shuteye

Beat number eight included the Columbia Restaurant. This is where I made good friends with a Puerto Rican and his son. They were janitors working there at the restaurant after hours.

Sometimes they would let me in and I would go upstairs to the room over the piazza which faced 7th Avenue.

It was there that I would sit on the thickly carpeted floor and "rest my eyes."

When the Sergeant was looking for me, they would cover for me, and tell him they couldn't speak English and he would leave. Then they would wake me up and let me out the back door into the alley.

Here we go with another Frank B. Woodlee story again. I was in the sandwich shop inside the Columbia restaurant which was visible from the sidewalk through a plate glass window. The Puerto Rican man and his son who worked as janitors in the restaurant by now allowed me free access whenever I desired. One night I was making use of this privilege to make Cuban sandwiches for the entire squad. Sgt. Woodlee (my much admired mentor) was driving down 7th Avenue checking on the welfare of his squad members when he observed me inside the restaurant. He aimed a spotlight at me and lit me up. He then gave me a look that clearly said: "What the heck are you doing?" and I simply signaled with my hands: "Do you want a small one or a big one?". He signaled back, "A big one" and we all ate well that night thanks to my Puerto Rican friends. I made Frank the largest one.

VIII

Mixing Friends & Agencies

Many of the persons that I talk about in these memories are still with us today. Many are not. Whether they are here or not, please know this. Each and every one of them holds a very special place in my heart. I am so very appreciative that they shared their lives with me.

(This section starts with another story featuring TPD Officer Cal Henderson and I.)

Officer Cal Henderson

While working together one night, Officer Cal Henderson and I spoke of how we both thought that the department was becoming very political.

We spoke of alternative openings for the two of us. Maybe we could switch over to the Federal side of law enforcement like the Border Patrol.

Cal suggested that Border Patrol wasn't a good fit for him because he couldn't speak any Spanish.

I assured Cal that the application has a portion which uses a different made up language which indicates whether or not the candidate could learn Spanish without much difficulty.

With that being said, we were off to the border. We filled out the application and we both passed.

He took the job and went. This momma's boy didn't.

Cal left and, before he returned to Tampa, he had served in both the Border Patrol as well as some stint involving the CIA.

After returning home, and marrying Sheriff Malcolm Beard's niece, he was hired on as a Deputy.

Cal was sharp! He scurried up the chain of command quicker than the mouse that ran up the clock.

Cal joined ranks with his friend "Tommy DePolis." They had known each other since their high school days at Chamberlain. Tommy became Cal's under Sheriff.

This was a great break for many young men and women who, through a good word from either of these fine police officers, started and enhanced their careers.

To this day these two gentlemen are revered in our law enforcing community.

Here are a few examples.

A bad traffic record as a heavy-footed teenager stopped one of my friends from becoming a Tampa Police Officer. He had a Master's Degree in Police Science.

One phone call to the right person accompanied by a sincere explanation and "bazinga!" A deputy sheriff was born.

After that, approximately a year later, another phone call was made, and in the wink of an eye, "bazinga!" A federal law enforcement officer was born.

Future Deputy

Try to digest this next example. A black female, five foot ten inches, one hundred and fifty to one hundred and sixty pounds working on her Master's Degree was sponsored to the Academy by our Tampa Police Department's Chief. We fast forward the story and find out that she couldn't get hired. Once again, with one phone call from the right person, "bazinga!" A female deputy sheriff appeared.

Deputy Kilbride

While on the Hillsborough County Sherriff's Office I encountered another endearing experience, which I will share next.

I grew up with a Deputy named "Kilbride." He was a big red headed Irishman who my parents were friends with early in life.

We met each other on the street about ten pm. Kilbride asked me where I was going after I got off. I responded, "home." Kilbride suggested that we go to a bottle club in Town n Country. I told Kilbride I was broke. He then handed me a twenty dollar bill and told me he'd meet me at the Dixie bottle club.

I met Kilbride in the parking lot of the club and we went for the entrance.

Upon opening the front door, I observed someone I knew professionally. He was a burglar and a maker of bombs. He was participating in a game of pool.

I didn't take another step. I motioned to Kilbride and handed my friend his twenty back.

I got in my car and went home, *where I belonged.*

Officer D. X. Tynan

Standing in formation in my first official roll call, I was behind an officer who had a different type of night stick on his gun belt. The chunk of wood appeared to have the shape of a pin used on ships to secure masts and sails in place.

Upon closer examination it appeared to have a furry surface. When viewed up close, that furry substance turned out to be blood and hair. This furry material was stuck in the cracks of the several pieces of wood that were doweled together that made up the night stick.

The wood used to make up the night stick is known as "iron wood." Interestingly enough, it is so hard that it is used to create ship bearings.

Officer D. X. was someone you truly wanted by your side when trouble came your way.

Unfortunately for us, later on in his career he was kind of forced out of the department over a supposed federal law violation involving the possession and sale of a fully automatic machine gun.

The purchaser had turned State's evidence in exchange for charges against them being dropped.

It was a very sad day for all involved.

Linda & Officer Peter Ambraz

Linda was a good looking brunette. She was the daughter of a Tampa Police Officer and a civilian who worked at 1710.

Linda caught the eye and apparently the heart of one Pete Ambraz. He was a tall, handsome officer who always treated everyone with the respect they deserved.

They made a great couple back then and are presently still together.

Officer Romeo Cole Junior

Romeo was another example of a family of father and son who both served at the same time on the force. I had the pleasure of working with them both. They were genuinely good folks.

Junior was working as a homicide detective and was riding with Jerry L. Feltman. (Feltman was a native of Hamilton Alabama and was a tall, wide. tough guy.)

At lunch one day, Romeo lamented about the venue chosen to enjoy lunch. Feltman responded to his lamentations with, "You pick the place."'

Romeo drove to Charley's Chicken Gizzard and asked Jerry what he liked on the menu. Feltman told Romeo, "Hell! I'll eat whatever you eat."

Romeo ordered two orders of rice and gravy with chitins. Feltman put a fork full in his mouth and kept chewing and chewing. But no matter how much he chewed, he was unable to swallow the delicious morsels.

Romeo handed Feltman a napkin and told him spit it out. Then said, "Hell, Charley. Bring this suffering "cracker" a cheeseburger.

Score: Feltman - zero; Cole - one.

Officer Ronnie Stroud

Ronnie was a colorful Tampa resident who was from a typical southern family. His father and brother were in the petroleum industry and they were obviously affluent.

Ronnie joined the department out of a personal desire to belong; and belong he did.

Stroud was well liked by everyone that he came in contact with.

In 1967, I received a call that there were gunshots being heard near the MacKay Bay incinerator south of Adamo Drive.

Upon arrival, I found Ronnie shooting a 30 caliber carbine at some waterfowl. He did this while standing in shallow water during low tide. This was not a real surprise.

Ronnie joined the Hillsborough County Sheriff's Office where he enjoyed a fruitful career. As I recall, Randy Latimer and Stroud were great friends and they both ended their careers as Hillsborough County Deputies.

Randy later on ventured into county politics and was successful in his endeavors.

Several other Tampa Police officers made the switch over to the HCSO for various

reasons. They all continued their stellar careers.

There was Ronnie Stroud, Stanley Guerra, Tommy DePolis , Robert Oates and a few others that I can't remember right now.

Oh! Let's not forget the two biggies, Walter Heinrich and Cal Henderson.

Officer Pilkay

Let's talk about Officer Pilkay a little bit.

He was a part of the machine gun episode mentioned earlier.

I will go over the case. We had a person who possessed the machine gun. We had the person who sold the machine gun. And finally, we had the third part of the puzzle. This was the person who purchased the illegal firearm.

This is a "who's on first" kind of situation.

Illegal guns could have become a problem for me as well. It wasn't, though, because the people involved in my scenario were tight-lipped and only a few select officers had any involvement with this particular event.

As before, we had a person who owned it, a person who possessed it, and one who sold it to another person. Our problem was that the person who sold it – *disappeared!*

I thank goodness for this "disappearance" for it could have been a sticky wicket for at least three of us.

Officer George Rotell

I just saw a little report about a friend of mine who had just passed away. I would not be happy with myself if I didn't mention this prince of a man.

Officer George Rotell was yet another transplant from up north. George was a medium framed man who was really too nice to be a police officer. You need certain traits to succeed in law enforcement.

Although George lacked the meanest of aggressions sometimes sought in an individual, he made up for this lacking with good traits.

When on the job, Officer Rotell was often assigned to drive the wagon or walk a two man beat. He was part of a squad of highly motivated, but sometimes mean, police officers who got the job done.

Let me share an example of this here.

This squad was comprised of guys like Jim Sigmon, Dick Cloud, me, and others. If you assaulted one of us, you might as well have assaulted us all.

This was an extremely bad mistake to make.

At about eighteen hundred hours one night, we were attempting to pull off an event that surely would have gotten us all in a little trouble with the sergeant if we got caught.

There were three of us traveling in individual one man units. We were all at the Goody Goody. This was the best drive thru in Tampa. They were well-known for their menu item which was southern fried chicken made to order. It took twenty to thirty minutes for them to prepare this culinary delight.

The problem was that Cloud, Sigmon, and I knew going to the Goody Goody and ordering that menu item was a no-no.

We took a chance anyway.

Just as the waitress was about to deliver the wonderful delight, two things occurred at the same time.

The first thing was a city garbage truck with trustees on board pulled onto the parking lot.

The second thing that occurred was this.

Officer Rotell was driving the paddy wagon in an alleyway just west of Nebraska Avenue. He radioed his call sign followed by 10-24. This was a call sign that told us all that a police officer's life is in immediate danger.

As a result of that call, the lucky trustees got our yummy fried chicken for free.

We dropped everything and all hauled butt to rescue our buddy, George.

Apparently George witnessed a woman walking down the alley being followed by a well-dressed older man who was shooting at her while following her.

We arrested him. It appears that he was a recently jilted lover and he wasn't very happy about the situation.

After the victim was stabilized, the ambulance driver tried to take her to the hospital for treatment.

The trip was bizarre. During the ride, the woman kept pulling off the sheet covering her naked body. She made most of the trip like she came into this world; butt naked.

The shooting originated in the man's new Cadillac. We caused some damage to the passenger's door retrieving the evidence.

The case was eventually dropped, but the city had to pay to have the old man's car fixed.

I should have stayed at the Goody Goody and eaten the yard bird.

Officer Ralph Rodriguez

One time, plain clothes Officer Ralph Rodriguez and I were at a bar on Gandy. It catered to military personnel because of its proximity to MacDill AF Base. Rodriguez was a Tampa native thought to be a quite handsome and suave Latin type.

While we were there, a US Marine was passed out on the bar. He had a stack of money in front of him.

Ralph and I observed the cute bar keeper taking this passed out drunk's cash every time someone would order a drink.

Not thinking that this was okay, I motioned her to the end of the bar and asked her to cease & desist that practice.

She asked me, "What are you going to do about it?"

I advised her that I was a police officer and that I would put her cute little ass in jail if she didn't comply.

Well, she thought she would leverage her situation by announcing my threat to the other male patrons who were benefiting from her activity.

Unfortunately for them, they thought that their testosterone was more potent than a squad of Tampa Police Officers.

So the fight was on.

Why not?

A torrential rain storm of beer & a wide variety of other liquids ensued as a result of this bar keeper's announcement.

Soon afterward, Papa Suave "Ralph" and I looked like two drowned rats. We won the battle but probably lost the war.

Officer Thomas R. Beury

At roll call one evening, I was assigned to ride with and also train a brand new police officer.

He was straight out of our in-house academy.

This young man's name was "Thomas R. Beury." His name plate read: T. R. BEURY.

He was a very nice but naive young man.

We rode many shifts together including day, evening and midnight shifts. We worked the north end near USF and also the south end of town south of Gandy Boulevard.

I'll tell a story involving him and will start with a midnight shift event.

I kept us out in the county during most of that shift. When we finally answered a call in our zone, Officer Beury asked in a loud voice, "Is this where we were supposed to be all week?"

One of the cutest stories involving T. R. was when I would hide in my own neighborhood. I'd lie in wait for my nineteen year old wife to go to work.

To her dismay, I would stop her, using red light and sirens, and embarrassing her to no end.

Tom thought doing this was just spiffy.

One time when I pulled her over she asked me what I would do if she took off her high heel shoe and hit me in the head with it.

I informed her that she probably would end up on my list of arrests for that day.

T.R. became pretty comfortable being my partner. A couple of days after I had pulled over my wife, he exclaimed "Joe, that yellow Volkswagen!"

I asked him, "What about it? Did it run a light or something?"

He told me, "No, but the driver sure was pretty!" T.R. sure knew how to pull me into things.

Enough said! On came our lights and siren and off we went.

I got out of the squad car and approached the driver. I asked the cutie pie for her license. The young lady inquired as to the reason I pulled her over.

I told her that my partner thought she was cute.

This lady's name was "Sherry."

It was soon after we pulled her over that she became Sherry Beury.

They have been married happily ever since, I hope.

Turnabout

Our unit had just made a drug arrest where a smart looking Corvette was confiscated during the arrest. A good looking Greek officer that I'll refer to as "George" (since I can't spell his last name) asked Captain Woodlee if he could drive it one night.

Woodlee gave the Greek permission and off he went.

The Captain wanted some company for his patrolling, so, I got to ride with the boss that night.

Radio advised us that one of our officers was requesting Captain Woodlee's presence north bound on I-275 over Sligh Avenue.

We discovered why when we got there.

The driver that was pulled over was none other than George the Greek and he was in the Corvette. He was being detained by a senior FHP State Trooper.

Of course, when you have an FHP pull over one of your people, you have to give him an opportunity to tell you how it occurred.

The trooper explained to us that he clocked our Greek officer going one hundred and thirty miles per hour. He said that he was going to place him under physical arrest and impound the Corvette.

George had told the trooper that he was working and on the way to meet an informant.

The trooper didn't move from his stance of arresting & impounding.

Woodlee thought for a minute. He then directed me to go and get a uniform traffic book. I did as he requested.

As I handed the book to Captain Woodlee, he told the trooper that if he persisted with this game we would join in as well.

Frank advised that FHP man that state statues prohibit anyone to leave a vehicle running while unattended.

Frank said, and I quote, "your fat ass is standing on the roadway and your cruiser is running unattended."

He continued with, "Go ahead, arrest my officer, and impound that car. The moment you go there, I will have Officer Severino arrest you and impound that State vehicle. Check mate, bubba!"

The FHP smiled as he closed his pad and wished us a most pleasant day.

Captain Whitehurst

Captain Whitehurst was a friend of Captain Woodlee. He had a real desire to succeed in life.

Whitehurst owned and operated an Ice Cream parlor located in a shopping center on the south end of town.

Woodlee helped Whitehurst get his Ice Cream Parlor set up. Woodlee and his brother were unlicensed contractors who were able to build anything. They prided themselves on their ability to build any structure, finishing with no more than a normal trash can load of scraps.

Jerry Woodlee was the manager of Duddy's Tire Company located in the heart of Ybor City south of 7th Avenue. Jerry kept us all in great tires for our own vehicles and at great prices throughout the years.

But what I want to share here relates to a burglary in progress in 1967 during an insurrection in Tampa.

In 1967 a mini riot was started in Tampa. It was started by a fellow police officer on our Squad named "Jim Calvert."

Officer Jim Calvert

It was during the day shift and it occurred in downtown Tampa. At that time, several youths had broken into a Camera shop and were running from the pursuing officers.

The culprits were running towards Central Park Projects where they resided. Officer Jim Calvert was a tall easy going police officer who was born in the Carolinas. Jim was easy going and not known for being a marksman by any stretch of the imagination. He was really more a fisherman.

We will discuss that soon. Let me focus back on the riot first.

Officer Calvert knew that he couldn't catch the thieves. He thought that if he took a shot at them maybe they would quit and give up.

He took the shot.

Unfortunately for the fifteen year old thief named "Martin Chambers," his body caught the only bullet fired. He got hit in the upper part of his young body and fell dead in mid stride.

It was in that moment that the city erupted. Both sides of the river separating the east side from west side were quite upset with what had occurred.

The mini riot continued for weeks. It caused most zone cars to be manned by three to four police officers.

This was not a good time to attract our attention in any way.

There were two not so smart known felons who decided in their infinite wisdom to take advantage of all the confusion. They chose to commit a burglary – *at Duddy's Tire Company!*

A uniformed patrol unit responded to the silent alarm. Officer Larry Lynch was one of the officers present from patrol. Several SEU units responded as backup including Johnny Ciccarello and I.

When we arrived, Larry Lynch stayed downstairs in the office. The building had two stories. The office was a room on the first floor with two of the walls of plate glass.

The west parking lot was visible from the office.

Officer Lynch was armed with a twelve gauge pump shotgun loaded and ready.

As the rest of us were searching for the bad guys, a Latin male named "Jarrez" jumped out the second floor window and landed in the grass just outside the office window.

Officer Lynch put the shotgun barrel against the glass and fired through the glass. He had seen Jarrez reach for a gun in his back pocket. Jarrez could not dodge the blast and he was severely wounded. He was rushed to Tampa General and expired later that night in its ICU.

The second suspect also jumped from a second story window. He lost his tennis shoe in this action and we took it as evidence.

The shoe had a special orthopedic built up inner sole. It was meant for someone with orthopedic problems.

Seeing the shoe, we almost all shouted in unison, "Hell! That's Cowboy Ippolito junior's shoe."

Officer Ciccarello then went to a phone and called the Ippolito household. He told them in

Italian that the police were coming after their son.

The big dummy ran out the front door right into our waiting arms.

I was later directed to go to Tampa General Hospital to check on the condition of the one suspect that had been shot. While walking thru ICU, I was scolded by a Pink Lady Volunteer to silence my loud radio and to speak softly. Hell, I was in intensive care!!

When I asked what condition Jarrez was in, the nurse's assistant asked me if he was a good guy or bad guy.

Upon seeing my negative response, she asked me if I wanted to see him die.

I shook my head up and down. With that motion from me, she reached over and unplugged the breathing bird.

His chest deflated.

She asked, "Do you want to see him come back to life?" She then reached over and plugged the bird back into the socket. His chest inflated once again.

Miraculous!

The Lure

One night after our shift was over, Jim was attempting to get someone to go fishing with him.

Jim was running out of people to ask, so he asked me. I told him I'd go but that I wasn't a very good fisherman.

He assured me I didn't need any skills.

This was right up my alley.

We met at the FOP, got in his pickup truck, and drove about two blocks away. We soon parked against the north curb of the Sligh Avenue Bridge.

Jim soon retrieved several Calcutta cane poles from the bed of his truck.

Now for you poor sportsmen out there, check this out. You might already know this trick. The poles were rigged with a length of stainless steel leader. It was inserted thru about four to five pieces of aluminum chair legs that had a hole drilled in the middle to allow the leader to be threaded through them where a four prong grappling hook attached.

Now here's the process. This setup was meant to work for only one species of salt water fish, the Snook.

The Snook is a very aggressive fish. It attacks noisy lures when they're put into the water and swirled in a figure eight motion. When the Snook attacks the lure, you snatch the fish out of the water and onto the street.

I looked over at Calvert and asked, "Ain't this lure illegal?"

Covert smiled and said, "We're cops! Who's gonna complain?"

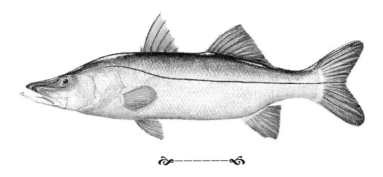

Rescues

My residence was at the intersection of 6th Street and Ballast Point Boulevard.

I was working the midnight shift in and around 34th Street and 9th Avenue. During this timeframe, companies with large fenced areas would contract with several other companies that, for a fee, would provide you with as many guard dogs as you desired.

Of course, the more dogs, the higher the bill.

HALT SUCKER!

The providing companies would bring their guard dogs to your property when you closed for the day and then come back and retrieve them in the morning before you opened for the day.

I recall that one of these companies was Protection Dogs Incorporated. Their office was on Busch Boulevard. It was owned by a pretty lady named "Linda" and her husband.

One night, I was looking down a street near these caged in areas and I observed a beautiful black German Shepherd sitting in the middle of the street wagging her tail. I decided to take a chance on getting bit. I got out of the car, opened the back door of my squad car and motioned for her to come to me.

This beautiful animal trotted over to my squad car and, without any hesitation, climbed into the back seat. I closed the door and drove home. When I got there, I gently picked up that beautiful girl and put her in my back yard.

I hurried back to my zone in Ybor city. I never spoke a word to anyone about my dog stealing that night.

I waited until seven-thirty that next morning to tell my wife about our new friend. At that time, I called her and told her about our new dog in our back yard.

I assured her that our new family member was very friendly.

I have always liked larger dogs; more especially unique breeds or colors. Black or white German Shepherds, Red Doberman Pinchers, and black Great Danes were my favorites.

One time, I bought a large black Dane from the son of a Tampa policeman Bill Bexley. The dog was enormous, but like most Danes, it was just a big furry baby that liked to get as much attention as possible.

Well, that and table scraps!

After coming home one morning from a midnight shift, I was getting ready to go to sleep when there was a knock at my door.

The knock was caused by a young man about eight years old. He was crying.

When I asked what was wrong, he said. "Your dog."

I asked him, "Did Baby bite you?"

He replied, "No sir. She stole my baseball."

I was very relieved. I let out a huge sigh and questioned him further.

It seems that when he walked up to our four foot chain link fence he leaned on the fence with his left hand. He had a baseball mitt on that hand which had a regulation hardball sitting in the web.

Well, Baby thought the kid wanted to play and that the ball he held up was offered to get the game going. She reached over the fence, took the ball in her mouth, and ran off.

When I called her to me, she had that baseball lodged firmly in her mouth and her mouth was completely closed. She was slobbering on the ball.

I carefully retrieved the ball, wiped it off, and returned it to a very happy little boy.

IX

The Beginning of The End

Swan Songs

Sergeant G.R. Smith wanted to work the upcoming concert at the Tampa Stadium. The entertainment scheduled that evening was going to be the famous *Led Zeppelin.*

George asked me to handle the squad and their assignments. Our squad was ordered to be on standby in case help was needed at the stadium.

The stage was already set up, the equipment was in place and thirty thousand or so tickets had been sold.

The crowds started to filter into the area. There were about one hundred to one hundred and fifty off-duty police officers there. They were more anxious to listen to the great entertainment and get paid than focus on the reason they were hired.

Just before the music was about to start, God started his own concert above us. He didn't skimp on the special effects either and used massive amounts of thunder & lightning in His own show.

The famous Led Zeppelin did not want to ruin their very expensive sound equipment. They packed up and hauled ass.

It was announced that the concert was cancelled and that Led Zeppelin had flown the coop.

Most of the disappointed attendees left pissed off but they left without much fuss.

Approximately five to ten thousand high or drunk spectators stayed with the intent of fighting to the end. They had planned to stay the duration and appeared to need some added incentive to move on.

Our squad was dispatched to help deal with this insurrection and provide any necessary leverage that could be legally provided.

Unfortunately for me, I had just washed my squad car and shined up the windows. They say if you want it to rain, clean your car!

As I drove onto the stadium property, I confronted a concert-goer who quickly hocked up a mouthful of luggie and spit it toward my face.

Fortunately, it hit the glass on my windshield, rebounded due to a God-provided stiff wind, and landed smack dab back in his face.

Shaking my head as I contained my laughter, I got out of my car. I was soon directed by a lieutenant to stop people from crossing the stadium property. We were being assaulted from both sides.

HALT SUCKER!

By now it was raining buckets. There were two guys and a girl kicking the filthy puddle water up and onto police officers as they stomped thru the mud, the shit, and the blood.

I ran up to the biggest one of the group and grabbed him around the neck. He was much stronger than I was and he twisted me to the left.

This one simple act further injured my already injured lower back and it irreversibly decided my future.

Man was I in pain!

I called out for help, and I heard someone yell back at me, "I'm coming, Guinea!"

I looked up and here comes Officer Michael "M. D." Smith.

Good Lord, was I glad to see him!

If you don't know what the MD stands for, I'm not going to tell you in this book.

Within a short period of time after this event, and at the insistence of the brass at the Tampa Police Department, I was examined for the last time by an orthopedic surgeon of their choosing who advised both parties that I was to retire because of the injuries received in the line of duty.

It was at that point in my career that I regretfully submitted my letter of retirement.

It was accepted by both the city and Fire & Police pension office.

The retirement became effective on 1 January 1978.

One More for the Road

On the lighter side of my career, there were several of us who were known for telling some great stories; some truthful, and some fictional.

Although Jim "Siggy" Simon was an artist in this area, I had a few of my own.

Here's an example of one of mine. It is the type of story we told each other and they evolved as a result of having far too many ears to tell it to.

I received a call to come into work one evening. It was unexpected. I was told that there was some type of insurrection unfolding.

As I drove off to respond to the situation, I noticed that I was driving on gas fumes.

If there's one thing I learned about department vehicles, it's that you never ever wanted them to run out of gas.

Why?

175

Because when you ran out of gas in a department vehicle, you automatically initiated a disciplinary order. And you never wanted to initiate something that you could avoid, *especially this!*

So, to avoid all that, I decided use $5.00 of my own money to make sure that I wouldn't run out of gas.

Fortunately, on my way to the station, there was a 7-Eleven. It was on the corner of Armenia Avenue and Buffalo Avenue.

I pulled up to the pump, parked, got out, and headed to the store to get the pump activated. On my way into the store to advise the clerk that I wanted to purchase five dollars' worth of gas for the car, I noticed that there was a large Rottweiler restrained with a heavy cow chain between two of the service bays. The dog must have weighed well over one hundred and twenty pounds.

As I looked over at him, the dog was drinking out of an old oil change can. It had a mixture of water, gas, and oil and had stained rags floating in the liquid mix. That was both disgusting to me and dangerous for the dog!

I made it a point to advise the station clerk of the dog's peril.

He just shrugged my comments off and told me to mind my own business.

You can imagine the thoughts I had going through my mind after receiving that response.

Realizing I had more pressing matters to attend to, I exited the office and headed back to my police vehicle.

As a passed by the dog once again, I heard a very recognizable "clunk, clunk, clunk." I knew that was the sound of trouble.

I looked over at that dog and I was right! That giant dog had broken that cow chain and now that 120 pound sharp-toothed machine was charging directly at me.

It was at that moment that I broke into a sprint and began an almost circular path around my police car.

Regrettably, the huge dog did the same and was gaining on me.

I did the only reasonable thing I could do in this situation and jumped onto the hood of my police car.

Unfortunately, the dog must have reasoned things out too and came to the same conclusion that I did. He was attempting to jump onto my hood as well.

So, I next climbed up onto the roof of the car. I felt that the two of us really needed our own space!

I was not sure as to what my next move was going to be.

I pulled out my Smith & Wesson thirty-eight revolver contemplating whether or not to shoot the animal.

While I was contemplating, that dog ran full speed around the car at least 3 to 4 more times. I'm absolutely positive that he was trying to figure out which area of the car he could access best to get onto the roof with me.

I was getting quite dizzy spinning around and keeping my eyes on him when all of a sudden, he collapsed on the pavement right in front of my car. He was absolutely motionless; not even a single muscle twitch!

I tell you, it was nerve-rackingly eerie to see his body so still like that!

Now, at this point, you might be tempted to ask the most obvious question that should come into your mind when you hear that a dog just stops like this.

What is that question?

"What happened to the dog? Did he die?"

And this is where I would tell whoever listened to this story and asked that most important question, "No! He just ran out of gas!"

Now, I've told this story to countless audiences over the years and usually with the same result. There is always one curious soul present that takes the bait, and the hook, the line, and the sinker as well.

Thanks for listening!

 ---- FINIS ----

Made in United States
Orlando, FL
14 December 2024